LAWS OF DUPLICATE CONTRACT BRIDGE

American Edition

As Promulgated in the Western Hemisphere by the
AMERICAN CONTRACT BRIDGE LEAGUE

Effective July 30, 1975

First Printing, June, 1975

Published by the American Contract Bridge League
Distributed by Crown Publishers, Inc., New York

First Printing, June 1975

Library of Congress Catalog Card Number: 75-16657

Dewey Classification 795.415

MADE IN THE UNITED STATES OF AMERICA

PREFACE TO THE AMERICAN EDITION

The first Laws of Duplicate Bridge were published in 1928, and revised in 1933. A further revision was made in 1935, and that edition was the first to receive official endorsement by a nationwide organization in the United States. The National Laws Commission was established, and all work on duplicate laws since that time has been conducted under its direction. The 1935 laws met with general acceptance, and no further revision was made until 1943.

During that period the Laws of Rubber Bridge had been promulgated by the Whist Club of New York in collaboration with the Portland Club of London. In 1947 an agreement was reached under which all law-making functions for both rubber bridge and duplicate bridge were consolidated in the American Contract Bridge League, which thereby became the sole American promulgating body. Three members of the Whist Club of New York were appointed to the National Laws Commission, which now functions as a committee of the American Contract Bridge League. The first duplicate laws published under this joint agreement were issued in 1949; and since they also had the collaboration of the Portland Club of London, the British Bridge League, and the European Bridge League, they became the first International Duplicate Contract Bridge Code. The same promulgating bodies issued the revised International Code of 1963.

The Laws of Duplicate Contract Bridge, 1975, as presented in this book supersede all of the above codes. In 1971, the World Bridge Federation established a W.B.F. Laws Commission (see page V, promulgating bodies); this is the first edition to carry the endorsement of that body, thus the first truly world-wide code.

This American edition is substantially identical to the new International Code; however, there is a considerable difference in form. Largely owing to the efforts of Donald Oakie, the Laws have been reorganized under many additional sub-headings, with the object of making it easier to find, in the table of contents, that provision of Law applicable to a particular case. The new format has necessitated occasional minor changes in wording, but in no instance is there a change of substance. This edition may be regarded as an "American translation" of the International Code.

The National Laws Commission acknowledges with thanks the assistance of Terry Smith, who acted as Secretary to the Drafting Committee, and to Alfred P. Sheinwold, Chairman of the National Laws Commission while this work was being done.

PROMULGATING BODIES

THE NATIONAL LAWS COMMISSION
of The American Contract Bridge League

EDGAR KAPLAN, *Chairman*

B. Jay Becker

John Gerber

Charles H. Goren

Thomas F. McCarthy

Carl B. Rubin

Easley Blackwood

Richard Goldberg

Oswald Jacoby

Donald Oakie

Edgar Theus

DRAFTING COMMITTEE
FOR DUPLICATE BRIDGE

ALFRED SHEINWOLD, *Chairman*

John Gerber

Donald Oakie

Edgar Kaplan

Edgar Theus

THE LAWS COMMISSION OF THE
WORLD BRIDGE FEDERATION

GEOFFREY L. BUTLER, *Chairman* (Great Britain)

Julius Rosenblum, *Ex-Officio* (U.S.A.)

Carlos Cabanne (Argentina)

Silvio Carini Mazzaccara (Italy)

Johannes Hammerich (Venezuela)

Edgar Kaplan (U.S.A.)

Andre LeMaitre (Belgium)

Dr. Ralph Mizroch (South Africa)

Donald Oakie (U.S.A.)

George Rosenkranz (Mexico)

Leslie Schneideman (New Zealand)

Alfred Sheinwold (U.S.A.)

Gunnar Zabel (Norway)

Victor Zirinsky (Hong Kong)

Contents

CHAPTER V — THE AUCTION

Part One — Correct Procedure

Section One — Auction Period

CONTENTS

CHAPTER X — TOURNAMENT DIRECTOR

Section One — Responsibilities

Section Two — Rulings

Section Three — Correction of Irregularities

Section Four — Penalties

CHAPTER XI — APPEALS

CONTENTS

The Scope of the Laws

The Laws are designed to define correct procedure and to provide an adequate remedy whenever a player accidentally, carelessly or inadvertently disturbs the proper course of the game, or gains an unintentional but nevertheless unfair advantage. An offending player should be ready to pay graciously any penalty or accept any adjusted score awarded by the Tournament Director.

The Laws are not designed to prevent dishonorable practices, but rather to redress damage inadvertently done.

The Object of the Proprieties

The object of the Proprieties is twofold: to familiarize players with the customs and etiquette of the game, generally accepted over a long period of years; and to enlighten those who might otherwise fail to appreciate when or how they are improperly conveying information to their partners — often a far more reprehensible offense than a violation of a law.

When these principles are appreciated, arguments are avoided and the pleasure that the game offers is materially enhanced.

The Scope of the Laws

The Object of the Prophecies

CHAPTER I

Definitions

Adjusted Score—An arbitrary score assigned by the Director (see Law 12).

Auction—1. The process of determining the contract by means of successive calls. 2. The aggregate of calls made. 3. The period during which calls are made.

Average—The arithmetic median between the greatest and least awarded scores available.

Bid—An undertaking to win at least a specified number of odd tricks in a specified denomination.

Board—A duplicate board as described in Law 2; or the four hands as originally dealt and placed in a duplicate board for play during that session.

Call—Any bid, double, redouble or pass.

Contestant—In an individual event, a player; in a pair event, two players playing as partners throughout the event; in a team event, four or more players playing as teammates.

Contract—The undertaking by declarer's side to win, at the denomination named, the number of tricks specified in the final bid, whether undoubled, doubled, or redoubled.

Convention—1. A call that serves by partnership agreement to convey a meaning not necessarily related to the denomination named. 2. Defender's play that serves to convey a meaning by agreement rather than inference.

Deal—1. The distribution of the pack to form the hands of the four players. 2. The cards so distributed considered as a unit, including the auction and play thereof.

1

Declarer—The player who, for the side that makes the final bid, first bid the denomination named in that bid. He becomes declarer when the auction is closed.

Defender—An opponent of declarer.

Denomination—The suit or notrump specified in a bid.

Director—A person designated to supervise a duplicate bridge contest and to apply these Laws.

Double—A call over an opponent's bid increasing the scoring value of fulfilled or defeated contracts (see Law 73).

Dummy—1. Declarer's partner. He becomes dummy when the auction is closed. 2. Declarer's partner's cards, once they are spread on the table after the opening lead.

Event—A contest of one or more sessions.

Follow Suit—Play a card of the suit that has been led.

Game—100 or more trick points scored on one deal.

Hand—The cards originally dealt to a player, or the remaining portion thereof.

Honor—Any Ace, King, Queen, Jack or ten.

International Match Point [*IMP*]—A unit of scoring awarded according to a schedule established in Law 74 B.

Irregularity—A deviation from the correct procedures set forth in the Laws and Proprieties.

Lead—The first card played to a trick.

Match Point—A unit of scoring awarded to a contestant as a result of comparison with one or more other scores.

Odd Trick—Each trick won by declarer's side in excess of six.

Opening Lead—The card led to the first trick.

Opponent—A player of the other side; a member of the partnership to which one is opposed.

Overtrick—Each trick won by declarer's side in excess of the contract.

Pack—The 52 playing cards with which the game of Contract Bridge is played.

Partner—The player with whom one plays as a side against the other two players.

Part Score—90 or fewer trick points scored on one deal.

Pass—A call specifying that a player does not, at that turn, elect to bid, double or redouble.

Penalty—An obligation or restriction imposed upon a side for violation of these Laws.

Penalty Card—A card prematurely exposed by a defender.

Play—1. The contribution of a card from one's hand to a trick, including the first card, which is the lead. 2. The aggregate of plays made. 3. The period during which the cards are played.

Premium Points—Any points earned other than trick points (see Law 73).

Rectification—Adjustment made to permit the auction or play to proceed as normally as possible after an irregularity has occurred.

Redeal—A second or subsequent deal by the same player to replace his first deal.

Redouble—A call that increases the scoring value of odd tricks or undertricks of a bid of one's own side that an opponent has doubled (see Law 73).

Revoke—The play of a card of another suit by a player who is able either to follow suit or to comply with a lead penalty.

Rotation—The clockwise order in which the right to call or play progresses.

Round—A part of a session played without progression of players.

Section—A group of contestants playing independently of any other group insofar as movement of boards and players is concerned.

Session—A period of play during which a specified number of boards is scheduled to be played.

Side—Two players who constitute a partnership against the other two players.

DEFINITIONS

Slam—A contract to win twelve tricks, six odd tricks (called Small Slam), or to win all thirteen tricks, seven odd tricks (called Grand Slam); also the fulfillment of such a contract.

Specified Suit—Any suit that a player, in exacting a penalty, requires to be led or not to be led.

Suit—One of four groups of cards in the pack, each group comprising thirteen cards and having a characteristic symbol: spades(♠), hearts(♡), diamonds(◇), clubs(♣).

Team—Two pairs playing in different directions at different tables, but for a common score (applicable regulations may permit teams of more than four members).

Trick—The unit by which the outcome of the contract is determined, regularly consisting of four cards, one contributed by each player in rotation, beginning with the lead.

Trick Points—Points scored by declarer's side for fulfilling the contract (see Law 73).

Trump—Each card of the suit, if any, named in the contract.

Turn—The correct time at which a player may call or play.

Undertrick—Each trick by which declarer's side falls short of fulfilling the contract (see Law 73).

Vulnerability—The condition of being exposed to greater undertrick penalties and entitled to greater premiums (see Law 73).

CHAPTER II

Preliminaries

LAW 1

THE PACK — RANK OF CARDS AND SUITS

Duplicate Contract Bridge is played with a pack of 52 cards, consisting of 13 cards in each of four suits. The suits rank downward in the order Spades(♠), Hearts(♡), Diamonds (♢), Clubs(♣). The cards of each suit rank downward in the order Ace, King, Queen, Jack, 10, 9, 8, 7, 6, 5, 4, 3, 2.

LAW 2

THE DUPLICATE BOARDS

A duplicate board containing a pack is provided for each deal to be played during a session. Each board is numbered and has four pockets to hold the four hands, designated North, East, South and West. The dealer and vulnerability are designated as follows:

North Dealer	Boards	1	5	9	13
East Dealer	Boards	2	6	10	14
South Dealer	Boards	3	7	11	15
West Dealer	Boards	4	8	12	16

Neither Side Vulnerable	Boards	1	8	11	14
North-South Vulnerable	Boards	2	5	12	15
East-West Vulnerable	Boards	3	6	9	16
Both Sides Vulnerable	Boards	4	7	10	13

The same sequence is repeated for Boards 17-32, and for each subsequent group of 16 boards.

LAW 3

ARRANGEMENT OF TABLES

Four players play at each table, and tables are numbered in a sequence established by the Director. He designates one direction as North; other compass directions assume the normal relationship to North.

LAW 4

PARTNERSHIPS

The four players at each table constitute two partnerships or sides, North-South against East-West. In pair or team events the contestants enter as pairs or teams, and retain the same partnerships throughout a session (except in the case of substitutions authorized by the Director). In individual events each player enters separately, and partnerships change during a session.

LAW 5

ASSIGNMENT OF SEATS

A. Initial Position

The Director assigns an initial position to each contestant (individual, pair or team) at the start of a session. Unless otherwise directed, the members of each pair or team may select seats, among those assigned to them, by mutual agreement. Having once selected a compass direction, a player may change it only upon instruction or permission of the Director.

B. Change of Direction or Table

Players change their initial compass direction or proceed to another table in accordance with the Director's instructions. The Director is responsible for clear announcement of instructions; each player is responsible for moving when and as directed, and for occupying the correct seat after each change.

CHAPTER III

Preparation and Progression

LAW 6

THE SHUFFLE AND DEAL

A. The Shuffle

Before play starts, each pack is shuffled. There must be a cut if either opponent so requests.

B. The Deal

The cards must be dealt face down, one card at a time in rotation, into four hands of thirteen cards each; each hand is then placed face down in one of the four pockets of the board.

C. Representation of Both Pairs at Deal

A member of each side must be present during the shuffle and deal unless the Director instructs otherwise.

D. New Shuffle and Redeal

1. Cards Incorrectly Dealt or Card(s) Exposed

There must be a new shuffle and a redeal if it is ascertained before the last card is dealt that the cards have been incorrectly dealt, or that a player has seen the face of a card.

2. At Director's Instruction

There must be a new shuffle and a redeal when required by the Director for any reason he deems sufficient.

E. Director's Option on Shuffling and Dealing
1. By Players
   The Director may instruct that the shuffle and deal be performed at each table immediately before play starts.
2. By Director
   The Director may perform the shuffle and deal in advance, himself.
3. By Agents or Assistants
   The Director may have his assistants, or other appointed agents, perform the shuffle and deal in advance.
4. Different Method of Dealing or Pre-dealing
   The Director may require a different method of dealing or pre-dealing.
F. Duplication of Board
   If required by the conditions of play, one or more exact copies of each original deal may be made under the Director's instructions.

LAW 7

CONTROL OF BOARDS AND CARDS

A. Placement of Board
   When a board is to be played it is placed in the center of the table. The board remains in the center of the table until play is completed.

B. Removal of Cards from Board

After the four players are seated, each player takes a hand from the pocket corresponding to his compass position.

1. Counting Cards in Hand before Play

    Each player must count his cards face down, before looking at the face of any card, to be sure he has exactly thirteen.

2. Control of Player's Hand

    During play each player retains possession of his own cards, not permitting them to be mixed with those of any other player. No player should touch any cards other than his own (but declarer may play dummy's cards in accordance with Law 45) during or after play except by permission of the Director.

3. Counting Cards in Hand after Play

    Each player should count his cards again after completion of play, just before returning them to the board.

C. Returning Cards to Board

Each player restores his original 13 cards to the pocket corresponding to his compass position. Thereafter no hand should be removed from the board unless a member of each side, or the Director, is present.

D. Responsibility for Procedures

The North player is responsible for the proper observance of these procedures, and for maintaining proper conditions of play at the table. However, if the East-West pair alone is stationary, the responsibility becomes East's.

LAW 8

SEQUENCE OF ROUNDS

A. Movement of Boards
   1. Director's Instructions
      At the start of each session, the Director instructs the players on the proper movement of boards from table to table at each round.
   2. Responsibility For Moving Boards
      The North player at each table is responsible for moving the boards just completed at his table to the proper table for the following round, unless the Director instructs otherwise.

B. End of Round
   In general, a round ends when the director gives the signal for the start of the following round; but if any table has not completed play by that time, the round continues for that table until play has been completed and the score of the final board of the round has been agreed upon and entered on the proper scoring form.

C. End of Last Round and End of Session
   The last round of a session, and the session itself, ends for each table when play of all boards scheduled at that table has been completed, and when all scores have been entered on the proper scoring forms.

CHAPTER IV

General Laws Governing Irregularities

LAW 9

PROCEDURE FOLLOWING AN IRREGULARITY

A. Calling Attention to an Irregularity
  1. During the Auction Period
     Any player may call attention to an irregularity during the auction, whether or not it is his turn to call.
  2. During the Play Period
     (a) Declarer or Either Defender
         Any of the three active players may call attention to an irregularity that occurs during the play period.
     (b) Dummy (dummy's restricted rights are defined in Laws 42 and 43).
         (1) Dummy may not call attention to an irregularity during the play but may do so after play of the hand is concluded.
         (2) Dummy may attempt to prevent an irregularity from occurring (Law 42B2).
B. After Attention is Called to an Irregularity
  1. Summoning the Director
     (a) When to Summon
         The Director must be summoned at once when attention is drawn to an irregularity.
     (b) Right to Summon
         Any player may summon the Director after attention has been drawn to an irregularity

during the auction. Any player except dummy may summon the Director during the play.

(c) Retention of Rights

Summoning the Director does not cause a player to forfeit any rights to which he might otherwise be entitled.

(d) Opponents' Rights

The fact that a player draws attention to an irregularity committed by his side does not affect the rights of the opponents.

2. Further Bids or Plays

No player should call or play until the Director has explained all matters in regard to rectification and to the assessment of a penalty.

C. Premature Correction of Irregularity

Any premature correction of an irregularity by the offender may subject him to a further penalty (see Law 26).

LAW 10

ASSESSMENT OF A PENALTY

A. Right to Assess Penalty

The Director alone has the right to assess penalties when applicable. Players do not have the right to assess or waive penalties on their own initiative.

B. Cancellation of Payment or Waiver of Penalty

The Director may allow or cancel any payment or waiver of penalties made by the players without his instructions.

C. Choice between Two or More Penalties
   1. Explanation of All Options
      When these laws provide an option among penalties, the Director explains all the options available.
   2. Declarer's Choice of Penalties
      If the declarer has a choice of penalties he must make his selection without assistance from dummy.

LAW 11

FORFEITURE OF THE RIGHT TO PENALIZE

A. Action by Non-Offending Side
   The right to penalize an irregularity may be forfeited if either member of the non-offending side takes any action before summoning the Director.
B. Action by Player to Offender's Left
   1. Call before Imposition of a Legal Penalty
      The right to penalize an irregularity is definitely forfeited if the player to offender's left calls, after an irregularity by his right hand opponent, and before a legal penalty has been stated and imposed (Law 34).
   2. Play before Imposition of a Legal Penalty
      The right to penalize an irregularity in play is definitely forfeited if the player to the offender's left plays, after the irregularity by his right hand opponent, before a legal penalty has been stated and imposed (Law 60).
C. Consultation between Non-Offending Partners
   1. Consultation Not Permitted
      Consultation between partners regarding the imposition of a penalty is not permitted.

2. Consultation Has Taken Place
   When the Director considers that the non-offending partners have consulted regarding the imposition of a penalty, the partnership forfeits its right to penalize.

D. Irregularity Called by Spectator
   1. Spectator Responsibility of Non-Offending Side
      The right to penalize an irregularity may be forfeited if attention is first drawn to the irregularity by a spectator for whose presence at the table the non-offending side is responsible.
   2. Spectator Responsibility of Offending Side
      The right to correct an irregularity may be forfeited if attention is first drawn to the irregularity by a spectator for whose presence at the table the offending side is responsible.

E. Penalty after Forfeiture of the Right to Penalize
   Even after the right to penalize has been forfeited under this law, the Director may assess a penalty under his exercise of discretionary powers.

LAW 12

DIRECTOR'S DISCRETIONARY POWERS

A. Right to Assign an Adjusted Score
   The Director may assign an adjusted score (or scores), either on his own initiative, or on the application of any player, but only when these Laws empower him to do so (see Law 84), or:

1. Laws Provide No Indemnity

   The Director may award an adjusted score when he judges that these Laws do not provide indemnity to the non-offending contestant for the particular type of violation of law or propriety committed by an opponent.

2. Normal Play of the Board Is Impossible

   The Director may assign an adjusted score if no rectification can be made that will permit normal play of the board.

3. Incorrect Penalty Has Been Paid

   The Director may assign an adjusted score if an incorrect penalty has been paid.

B. No Adjustment for Undue Severity of Penalty

   The Director may not assign an adjusted score on the ground that the penalty provided in these Laws is either unduly severe or advantageous to either side.

C. Assignment of Adjusted Score

   1. How Assigned

      An adjusted score is assigned by altering the total-point score on the board prior to matchpointing, or by the assignment of zero or more match points (see Law 84).

   2. Point Assignment in Proportion to Irregularity

      (a) Point Award to Non-Offending Side

          The number of points assigned to the non-offending side should not exceed the number required to offset the irregularity.

      (b) Points Assigned to Offending Side

          The number of points assigned to the offending side to offset the irregularity may be reduced by penalty points.

   3. Balance in Assigned Scores

      The indemnity points awarded the non-offending side need not balance the penalty points assessed against the offending side.

LAW 13

INCORRECT NUMBER OF CARDS

A. No Player Has Seen Another Player's Card(s)

When the Director decides that one or more pockets of the board contained an incorrect number of cards, he should correct the discrepancy as follows and require that the board then be played and scored normally.

1. Hand Records

    When hand records are available, the Director should distribute the cards in accordance with the records.

2. Consult Previous Players

    If hand records are not available, the Director should correct the board by consulting with players who have previously played it.

3. Require a Redeal

    If the board was incorrectly dealt, the Director should require a redeal (Law 6).

B. A Player Has Seen Another Player's Card(s)

When the Director determines that one or more pockets of the board contained an incorrect number of cards, and after restoration of the board to its original condition a player has seen one or more cards in another player's hand, if the Director deems:

1. The Information Gained Is Inconsequential

    That such information will not interfere with normal bidding or play, the Director should require that the board be played and scored normally.

2. The Information Will Interfere with Normal Play

    That the information gained thereby is of sufficient importance to interfere with normal play, the Director should award an adjusted score and may penalize an offender.

LAW 14

MISSING CARD

A. Hand Found Deficient Before Play Commences

When three hands are correct and the fourth is found to be deficient before the play period begins, the Director makes a search for the missing card, and:

1. Card Is Found

   If the card is found, it is restored to the deficient hand.

2. Card Cannot Be Found

   If the card cannot be found, the Director reconstructs the deal, as near to its original form as he can determine, by substituting another pack.

B. Hand Found Deficient During Play

When three hands are correct and the fourth is found to be deficient during play, the Director makes a search for the missing card, and:

1. Card Is Found

   (a) If the card is found among the played cards, Law 67 applies.

   (b) If the card is found elsewhere, it is restored to the deficient hand, and penalties may apply (see 3., following).

2. Card Cannot Be Found

   If the card cannot be found, the deal is reconstructed as nearly as can be determined in its original form by substituting another pack; and penalties may apply (see 3., following).

3. Possible Penalties

   A card restored to a hand under the provisions of Section B of this Law is deemed to have belonged continuously to the deficient hand. It may become a penalty card (Law 50), and failure to have played it may constitute a revoke.

LAW 15

PLAY OF A WRONG BOARD

A. Players Have Not Previously Played Board
   If players play a board not designated for them to play
   in the current round:
   1. Designate a Late Play
      The Director may require both pairs to play the
      correct board against each other later.
   2. Score Board as Played
      The Director should allow the score to stand if none of
      the four players have previously played the board.
B. One or More Players Have Previously Played Board
   If any player plays a board he has previously played,
   with the correct opponents or otherwise, his second
   score on the board is cancelled both for his side and his
   opponents', and the Director should award an adjusted
   score to the contestants deprived of the opportunity to
   earn a valid score.

LAW 16

UNAUTHORIZED INFORMATION

A. Definition
   1. Accidental Unauthorized Information
      Any extraneous information a player receives about
      a board he is playing or has yet to play is accidental.
      This unauthorized information encompasses informa-
      tion received by looking at the wrong hand; by
      overhearing calls, results or remarks; by seeing
      cards at another table, or by seeing a card belonging
      to another player at one's own table before the
      auction begins.

2. Illegal Unauthorized Information

Any information conveyed by a player, other than declarer, to his partner by means of a remark, question, unmistakable hesitation, special emphasis, tone, gesture, movement, mannerism, or any other action that may suggest a call, lead or plan of play, is illegal unauthorized information.

B. Report of Accidental Unauthorized Information

The Director should be notified forthwith of the accidental receipt of any unauthorized information, preferably by the recipient.

1. Director's Action

(a) Board Can Be Played Normally

If the Director judges that the unauthorized information accidentally received is not of sufficient importance to interfere with normal bidding or play, he should require that the board be played and scored normally.

(b) Board Cannot Be Played Normally

If the Director judges that the board cannot be played normally:

(1) Award Adjusted Score

The Director may assign an adjusted score to the pairs involved; or

(2) Substitute Player

The Director may appoint a temporary substitute to replace the player who received unauthorized information.

C. Report of Alleged Illegal Information

1. Calling the Director

Any player except dummy may call the Director if it appears that illegal information has been conveyed by another player.

2. Director's Action

If attention is drawn to the offense and the Director is summoned forthwith, the Director should require that the auction or play continue, reserving his right to assign an adjusted score if he considers that the result could have been affected by the illegal information.

CHAPTER V

The Auction

PART I

CORRECT PROCEDURE

SECTION ONE

AUCTION PERIOD

LAW 17

DURATION OF THE AUCTION

A. **Auction Period Starts**
   The auction period begins for each player when he looks at his hand after removing it from the board.

B. **The First Call**
   The player designated by the board as dealer makes the first call.

C. **Successive Calls**
   The player to dealer's left makes the second call, and thereafter each player calls in turn in a clockwise rotation.

D. **End of Auction Period**
   The auction period ends when three passes in rotation have followed any call (but see Law 35).

LAW 18

BIDS

A. Proper Form

A bid must name a number of odd tricks, from one to seven, and a denomination. (Pass, double and redouble are calls but not bids.)

B. To Supersede a Bid

A bid supersedes a previous bid if it names either the same number of odd tricks in a higher-ranking denomination, or a greater number of odd tricks in any denomination.

C. Sufficient Bid

A bid that supersedes the immediately previous bid is a sufficient bid.

D. Insufficient Bid.

A bid that fails to supersede the immediately previous bid is an insufficient bid.

E. Rank of the Denominations .

The rank of the denominations in descending order is: notrump, spades, hearts, diamonds, clubs.

LAW 19

DOUBLES AND REDOUBLES

A. Doubles

1. Legal Double

A player must double only the last preceding bid. The bid must have been made by an opponent and no calls other than pass may have intervened.

2. Proper Form for Double

   In doubling, a player should not state the number of odd tricks or the denomination. The only correct form is the single word "Double".

3. Double of Incorrectly Stated Bid

   If a player, in doubling, incorrectly states the bid, or the number of odd tricks or the denomination, he is deemed to have doubled the bid as it was made. (Law 16 — Unauthorized Information — may apply.)

B. Redoubles

   1. Legal Redouble

      A player may redouble only the last preceding double. The double must have been made by an opponent and no calls other than pass may have intervened.

   2. Proper Form for a Redouble

      In redoubling a player should not state the number of odd tricks or the denomination. The only correct form is the single word "Redouble".

   3. Redouble of an Incorrectly Stated Bid

      If a player, in redoubling, incorrectly states the doubled bid, or the number of odd tricks or the denomination, he is deemed to have redoubled the bid as it was made. (Law 16 — Unauthorized Information — may apply.)

C. Double or Redouble Superseded

   Any double or redouble is superseded by a subsequent legal bid.

D. Scoring a Doubled or Redoubled Contract

   If a doubled or redoubled bid is not superseded by a subsequent legal bid, scoring values are increased as provided in Law 73.

LAW 20

REVIEW AND EXPLANATION OF CALLS

A. Call Not Clearly Heard
   A player who does not hear a call distinctly may forthwith require that it be repeated.

B. Review of Auction during Auction Period
   Before the auction closes, a player is entitled to have all* previous calls restated when it is his turn to call, unless he is required by law to pass.

C. Review after Close of Auction
   1. Opening Lead Inquiry
      After the final pass either defender has the right to ask if it is his opening lead (see Laws 47 E and 41).
   2. Review of Auction
      Declarer or either defender may, at his first turn to play, require all* previous calls to be restated.

D. Who May Review the Auction
   A request to have calls restated should be responded to only by an opponent.

E. Correction of Error in Review
   Any player, including dummy or a player required by law to pass, may and should promptly correct an error in restatement.

F. Explanation of Conventional Meaning of Calls
   1. During the Auction
      During the auction and before the final pass, a full explanation of any call made by an opponent may be requested by any player, but only at that player's turn to call.

---

*A player may not ask for a partial restatement of previous calls and should not halt the review before it has been completed.

2. During the Play Period

    After the final pass and throughout the play period, declarer or either defender* may request such an explanation of opposing calls, and declarer may request an explanation of the defenders' card play conventions, but only at his own turn to play (N.B.: Law 16 may apply).

LAW 21

CALL BASED ON MISINFORMATION

A. Call Based on Caller's Misunderstanding

   A player has no recourse if he has made a call on the basis of his own misunderstanding.

B. Call Based on Misinformation from an Opponent

   1. Change of Call

      A player may, without penalty, change a call he may have made as a result of misinformation given to him by an opponent (failure to alert promptly to a conventional call or special understanding, where such alert is required by the sponsoring organization, is deemed misinformation), provided that his partner has not subsequently called.

   2. Change of Call by Opponent Following Correction

      When a player elects to change a call because of misinformation (as in 1., preceding), his left hand opponent may then in turn change any subsequent call he may have made, without penalty (unless his withdrawn call conveyed such substantial information as to damage the non-offending side, in which case the Director may assign an adjusted score).

----

*Sponsoring organizations are specifically authorized to establish different regulations applying to the defenders' questions before the first trick has been completed.

3. Too Late to Change Call
   When it is too late to change a call, Law 40C may apply.

SECTION TWO

AUCTION IS CLOSED

LAW 22

PROCEDURE AFTER THE AUCTION IS CLOSED

A. No Player Has Bid
   After the aucton is closed, if no player has bid, the hands are returned to the board without play. There may not be a redeal.
B. One or More Players Have Bid
   If any player has bid, the final bid becomes the contract and play begins.

PART II

IRREGULARITIES IN PROCEDURE

SECTION ONE

EXPOSED CARD, AUCTION PERIOD

LAW 23

CARD EXPOSED OR LED DURING AUCTION

A. Director's Action

When the Director determines, during the auction, that a player has faced a card on the table, or held a card so that it is possible for his partner to see its face, he must require that every such card be left face up on the table until the auction closes; and (penalty) if the offender subsequently becomes a defender, declarer may treat every such card as a penalty card (Law 50). In addition:

1. Low Card Not Prematurely Led

   If it is a single card below the rank of an honor and not prematurely led, there is no further penalty.

2. Single Card of Honor Rank, or Card Prematurely Led

   If the card is a single card of honor rank, or is any card prematurely led, (penalty) offender's partner must pass when next it is his turn to call.

3. Two or More Cards are Exposed

   If two or more cards are so exposed, (penalty) offender's partner must pass when next it is his turn to call.

B. Enforced Pass May Damage Innocent Side

When the penalty for an irregularity, under this or any other Law, would compel the offender's partner to pass at his next turn, and when the Director deems that this enforced pass will necessarily damage the innocent side:

1. Direct That the Auction Continue

    The Director may direct that the auction and play continue, reserving the right to assign an adjusted score if he considers that the result was affected by the illegal information, or:

2. Assign an Adjusted Score

    The Director may forthwith assign an adjusted score.

SECTION TWO

CHANGES OF CALLS

LAW 24

IMMEDIATE CORRECTION OF CALL

A. Correcting Inadvertent Call

A player may substitute his intended call for an inadvertent call but only if he does so, or attempts to do so, without pause for thought. If legal, his last call stands without penalty.

B. Correction to an Illegal Call

If the substituted call is an illegal call, it is subject to the applicable Law.

LAW 25

CHANGE OF CALL

A. Attempt to Change Illegal Call
   A call substituted for an illegal call made previously at the same turn, when too late for correction as provided in Law 24, is cancelled. The offending side is subject to the applicable law for the illegal call, and may also be subject to Law 26.

B. Attempt to Change Legal Call
   A call substituted for a legal call made previously at the same turn, when Law 24 does not apply, is cancelled. The legal call stands and (penalty):

   1. Auction Period Penalty
      The offender's partner must pass whenever it is his turn to call.
   2. Lead Penalties
      Offender's partner may be subject to the lead penalties of Law 26.

LAW 26

UNAUTHORIZED INFORMATION GIVEN BY CHANGE OF CALL

When a player illegally names a denomination not selected as his final call at that turn (as in changing a call except as permitted by Law 24, or in making or correcting a legal call), then if he becomes a defender:

A. Illegal Call Is a Suit Bid
   If the illegal call is a suit bid:
   1. Illegally Named Suit Is Not Conventional

    (a) Require Lead of Illegally Named Suit

        Require the offender's partner to lead the illegally named suit at his first turn to lead (including the opening lead); or

    (b) Prohibit Lead of Illegally Named Suit

        Prohibit the offender's partner from leading the illegally named suit at his first turn to lead (including the opening lead) and for as long as the offender's partner retains the lead.

  2. Illegally Named Suit Is Conventional

    When the illegally named suit is conventionally related to another suit or suits, declarer may either (penalty):

    (a) Require Lead of Conventionally Related Suit

        Require the offender's partner to lead a card of a specified suit thus conventionally related at his first turn to lead (including the opening lead); or

    (b) Prohibit Lead of Conventionally Related Suit

        Prohibit the offender's partner from leading any card of any thus related suit at his first turn to lead (including the opening lead) and for as long as the offender's partner retains the lead.

B. Illegal Call Is Notrump Bid

  If the illegal call was a notrump bid,

  1. Notrump Bid Is Not Conventional

    When the illegal notrump bid is not conventionally related to a suit or suits, and if the offender's partner is to make the opening lead, (penalty) declarer may require the offender's partner to make the opening lead in a specified suit.

  2. Notrump Bid Relates to Suit or Suits

    When the illegal notrump bid conventionally relates to a suit or suits, Law 26A2 applies.

C. Illegal Double or Redouble

  If another call has been substituted for an illegal double or redouble, the penalties provided in Law 27B3 apply.

SECTION THREE

INSUFFICIENT BID

LAW 27

INSUFFICIENT BID

A. Insufficient Bid Accepted

Any insufficient bid may be accepted (treated as legal) at the option of the opponent to offender's left. It is accepted if that player calls.

B. Insufficient Bid Not Accepted

If an insufficient bid made in rotation is not accepted, it must be corrected by the substitution of either a sufficient bid or a pass (the offender is entitled to select his final call at that turn after the applicable penalties have been stated, and any call he has previously attempted to substitute is cancelled, but Law 26 may apply).

1. Corrected by Lowest Sufficient Bid in Same Denomination

   (a) No Penalty

   If the insufficient bid is corrected by the lowest sufficient bid in the same denomination, the auction proceeds as though the irregularity had not occurred (but see (b) following).

   (b) Award of Adjusted Score

   If the Director judges that the insufficient bid conveyed such substantial information as to damage the non-offending side, he may assign an adjusted score.

2. Corrected by Any Other Sufficient Bid

   If the insufficient bid is corrected by any other

sufficient bid, (penalty) the offender's partner must pass whenever it is his turn to call (and Law 26 may apply).

3. Corrected by a Pass

If the insufficient bid is corrected by a pass, (penalty) the offender's partner must pass whenever it is his turn to call; and if the offender's partner is to make the opening lead:

(a) **Require Lead of Specified Suit**

Declarer may require the offender's partner to lead a specified suit; or

(b) **Prohibit Lead of a Specified Suit**

Declarer may prohibit the offender's partner from leading a specified suit; this prohibition to continue for as long as offender's partner retains the lead.

4. Attempt to Correct by a Double or Redouble

If the offender attempts to substitute a double or redouble for his insufficient bid, the attempted call is cancelled; he must pass and the offense (penalty) is subject to the penalties provided in (3) preceding.

C. Insufficient Bid Out of Rotation

If a player makes an insufficient bid out of rotation, Law 31 applies.

SECTION FOUR

CALL OUT OF ROTATION

LAW 28

CALLS CONSIDERED TO BE IN ROTATION

A. Right Hand Opponent Required to Pass
   A call is considered to be in rotation when it is made by a player at his right hand opponent's turn to call, if that opponent is required by law to pass.

B. Call By Correct Player Cancelling Call Out of Rotation
   A call is considered to be in rotation when made by a player whose turn it was to call, before a penalty has been assessed for a call out of rotation by an opponent; the call thus made waives any penalty for the call out of rotation and the auction proceeds as though the opponent had not called at that turn.

LAW 29

PROCEDURE AFTER A CALL OUT OF ROTATION

A. Out of Rotation Call Cancelled
   A call out of rotation is cancelled (but see B following) and the auction reverts to the player whose turn it was to call. Offender may make any legal call in proper rotation, but may be subject to penalty under Laws 30, 31 or 32.

B. Forfeiture of Right to Penalize
   Following a call out of rotation, the opponent next in rotation to the offender may elect to call, thereby forfeiting the right to penalize.

LAW 30

PASS OUT OF ROTATION

A. Before Any Player Has Bid

When a player has passed out of rotation before any player has bid, (penalty) the offender must pass when next it is his turn to call.

B. After Any Player Has Bid

1. At Offender's Right Hand Opponent's Turn to Call

After any player has bid, for a pass out of rotation made at the turn of offender's right hand opponent to call, (penalty) offender must pass when next it is his turn to call (if the pass out or rotation relates by convention to a specific suit, or suits, thereby conveying information, Law 26 may apply).

2. At Offender's Partner's Turn to Call

(a) Action Required of Offender

After any player has bid, for a pass out of rotation made at the offender's partner's turn to call, (penalty) the offender must pass whenever it is his turn to call (and Law 26 may apply).

(b) Action Open to Offender's Partner

Offender's partner may make any sufficient bid, or may pass, but may not double or redouble at that turn.

(c) Offender's Partner Passes

If offender's partner passes and subsequently is to make the opening lead:

(1) Require Lead of a Specified Suit

Declarer may require offender's partner to lead a specified suit; or

(2) Prohibit Lead of a Specified Suit

Declarer may prohibit offender's partner from leading a specified suit, such prohibition to continue for as long as he retains the lead.

3. At Offender's Left Hand Opponent's Turn to Call
   After any player has bid, a pass out of rotation at
   offender's left hand opponent's turn to call is treated
   as a change of call and Law 25 applies.

LAW 31

BID OUT OF ROTATION

When a player has bid out of rotation (and the bid is cancelled, as the option to accept the bid has not been exercised
— see Law 29):

A. Before Any Player Has Called
   1. Offender's Right Hand Opponent's Turn to Call
      (a) Right Hand Opponent Passes
          When his right hand opponent passes, offender
          must repeat the bid out of rotation and there is no
          penalty.
      (b) Right Hand Opponent Bids
          If his right hand opponent bids, offender may
          pass or make any legal bid; if his bid
          (1) Repeats Denomination of Bid Out of Rotation
              Repeats the denomination of his bid out of
              rotation, (penalty) offender's partner must
              pass when next it is his turn to call (see
              Law 23 B).
          (2) Does Not Repeat Denomination of Bid Out Of
              Rotation
              Names a denomination other than that named
              in his call out of rotation, (penalty) offender's
              partner must pass whenever it is his turn to
              call (see Law 23 B) and Law 26 may apply.

2. Offender's Partner's or Left Hand Opponent's Turn to Call

When a player has bid out of rotation, and it was the turn of either his partner or his left hand opponent to call, (penalty) offender's partner must pass whenever it is his turn to call (see Law 23 B), and Law 26 may apply.

B. After Any Player Has Called
  1. At Offender's Partner's Turn to Call
  When a player has bid out of rotation, after any player has called, and when it was offender's partner's turn to call, (penalty) offender's partner must pass whenever it is his turn to call (see Law 23 B), and Law 26 may apply; and if offender's partner is to make the opening lead:
    (a) Requiring the Lead of a Specified Suit
    Declarer may require offender's partner to lead a specified suit; or
    (b) Prohibiting the Lead of a Specified Suit
    Declarer may prohibit offender's partner from leading a specified suit, such prohibition to continue for as long as he retains the lead.
  2. At Offender's Right Hand Opponent's Turn to Call
    (a) Right Hand Opponent Passes
      (1) Out of Rotation Bid Was Sufficient
      If the bid out of rotation was sufficient, and offender's right hand opponent now passes, offender must repeat his bid and there is no penalty.
      (2) Out of Rotation Bid Was Insufficient
      If the bid out of rotation was insufficient, and offender's right hand opponent now passes, offender's insufficient bid must be corrected as though it had been made in rotation, as provided in Law 27.

  (b) Right Hand Opponent Makes a Legal Bid, Double
    or Redouble*
    If offender's right hand opponent makes a legal
    bid, double or redouble, (penalty) the penalty
    provisions of 'A1(b)' preceding apply.

 3. At Offender's Left Hand Opponent's Turn to Call
  Offender's bid out of rotation is treated as a change of
  call and Law 25 applies.

LAW 32

DOUBLE OR REDOUBLE OUT OF ROTATION

A. Inadmissible Double or Redouble Out of Rotation
 An inadmissible double or redouble out of rotation is
 subject to Law 36.

B. Double or Redouble Out of Rotation, in Violation of
 Obligation to Pass
 A double or redouble out of rotation when in violation of
 a legal obligation to pass, is subject to Law 37.

C. Doubles or Redoubles Out of Rotation Not Subject to
 Laws 36 or 37.

 1. Made at Offender's Partner's Turn to Call
  If a double or redouble out of rotation has been
  made when it was the offender's partner's turn to
  call, the offender's partner must pass whenever it is
  his turn to call (see Law 23 B); the offender may not
  thereafter, in turn, double or redouble the same
  bid he doubled or redoubled out of turn; and if the
  offender's partner is to make the opening lead:

  (a) Requiring the Lead of a Specified Suit
    Declarer may require the offender's partner to
    lead a specified suit; or

---

*An illegal call by that opponent may be penalized in the usual way, after
which this subsection 'B2(b)' applies.

(b) Prohibiting the Lead of a Specified Suit

Declarer may prohibit the offender's partner from leading a specified suit, such prohibition to continue for as long as the offender's partner retains the lead.

2. Made at Offender's Right Hand Opponent's Turn to Call

If a double or redouble out of rotation has been made at offender's right hand opponent's turn to call, then:

(a) Offender's Right Hand Opponent Passes

If offender's right hand opponent passes, offender must repeat his out of rotation double or redouble and there is no penalty.

(b) Offender's Right Hand Opponent Bids

If offender's right hand opponent bids, the offender may in turn make any legal call and the penalty provisions of 27B3 apply.

LAW 33

SIMULTANEOUS CALLS

A call made simultaneously with one made by the player whose turn it was to call, is deemed to be a subsequent call.

LAW 34

CALL IN ROTATION AFTER AN ILLEGAL CALL

A. Forfeiture of Penalty For Illegal Call

A call by a member of the non-offending side, after an illegal call by the opponent to his right, and before a penalty has been assessed, forfeits the right to penalize the offense.

B. Illegal Call Legalized

The illegal call is treated as though it were legal, except that:

1. Illegal Call Was a Bid of More Than Seven

   A bid of more than seven is treated as a pass.

2. Illegal Call Was an Inadmissible Double or Redouble

   If the illegal call was an inadmissible double or redouble, that call and all subsequent calls are cancelled; the auction reverts to the player whose turn it was to call and proceeds as though there had been no irregularity. Law 35 or 37 may apply.

LAW 35

RETENTION OF RIGHT TO CALL

A. Player Retains Right to Call

A player may not be deprived of his right to call by one or more passes following a pass out of rotation, when there has been no subsequent bid.

B. Passes Cancelled

The Director should cancel all such passes, and the bidding reverts to the player who had missed his turn. The auction proceeds as though there had been no irregularity.

SECTION FIVE

INADMISSIBLE CALLS

LAW 36

INADMISSIBLE DOUBLE OR REDOUBLE

A. Definition

An inadmissible double or redouble is one not permitted by Law 19.

B. Inadmissible Double or Redouble Cancelled

Any inadmissible double or redouble is cancelled, and the offender must substitute a legal call; Law 26 applies.

C. Inadmissibly Doubled or Redoubled Bid Becomes Final Contract

If the bid that was inadmissibly doubled or redoubled becomes the final contract, either member of the non-offending side may specify that the contract be played undoubled.

D. Right to Penalize Inadmissible Double or Redouble is Forfeited

If the right of the non-offending side to penalize is forfeited, Law 34 applies.

LAW 37

BID, DOUBLE OR REDOUBLE IN VIOLATION OF OBLIGATION TO PASS

A. Bid, Double or Redouble Cancelled

If a player required by law to pass bids, doubles or redoubles, his call is cancelled, and:

1. Auction Penalty

   Both members of the offending side must pass during the remainder of the auction.

2. Lead Penalties

   If the offender's partner is to make the opening lead,

   (a) Require Lead of Specified Suit

   Declarer may require offender's partner to lead a specified suit; or

   (b) Prohibit Lead of Specified Suit

   Declarer may prohibit offender's partner from leading a specified suit, such prohibition to continue for as long as offender's partner retains the lead.

B. Right To Penalize Forfeited

   If the right of the non-offending side to penalize is forfeited as provided in Law 11, the offender's bid, double or redouble, if otherwise legal, stands at that turn; but if the offender was required to pass for the remainder of the auction, he must still pass at subsequent turns.

LAW 38

BIDS OF MORE THAN SEVEN

No play or score at a contract of more than seven is ever permissible.

A. Bid of More Than Seven Cancelled

   A bid of more than seven by any player is cancelled, and (penalty) both members of the offending side must pass during the remainder of the auction.

B. Lead Penalty

   If a player bids more than seven, and his partner is to make the opening lead, declarer may either;

   1. Require Lead of a Specified Suit

      Require offender's partner to lead a specified suit; or

2. Prohibit Lead of Specified Suit

   Prohibit offender's partner from leading a specified suit, such prohibition to continue for as long as offender's partner retains the lead.

C. Right to Penalize Forfeited

   If the right to penalize is forfeited as provided in Law 11, the offender must substitute a pass; any call that may have been made subsequently is cancelled; and the auction proceeds as though there had been no irregularity.

LAW 39

CALL AFTER THE AUCTION IS CLOSED

A. Call after Auction Ends

   A call made after the auction is closed is cancelled.

B. Pass by Defender

   If a defender passes after the auction is closed there is no penalty.

C. Any Call by Declarer or Dummy

   If declarer or dummy makes any call after the auction is closed there is no penalty.

D. Bid, Double or Redouble by a Defender

   If a defender bids, doubles or redoubles after the auction is closed, declarer may either:

   1. Require Lead of Specified Suit

      Require offender's partner, when first it is his turn to lead, to lead a specified suit; or

   2. Prohibit Lead of Specified Suit

      Prohibit offender's partner, when first it is his turn to lead, from leading a specified suit, such prohibition to continue for as long as the offender's partner retains the lead.

E. Right to Penalize Forfeited

If the right of the non-offending side to penalize is forfeited, as provided in Law 11, all calls made after the close of the auction are cancelled without penalty.

SECTION SIX

CONVENTIONS AND AGREEMENTS

LAW 40

PARTNERSHIP UNDERSTANDINGS

A. Right to Call

A player may make any call or play (including an intentionally misleading call — such as a 'psychic' bid — or a call or play that departs from commonly accepted, or previously announced, conventional practice), without prior announcement, provided that such call or play is not based on a partnership understanding.

B. Concealed Partnership Understandings Prohibited

A player may not make a call or play based on a partnership understanding, unless an opposing pair may reasonably be expected to understand its meaning, or unless his side discloses the use of such call or play in accordance with the regulations of the sponsoring organization.

C. Director's Option

If the Director decides that a side has been damaged through its opponents' failure to explain the meaning of a call or play, he may award an adjusted score.

D. Regulation of Conventions
    The sponsoring organization may regulate the use of
    bidding or play conventions.

E. Convention Card
    1. Right to Prescribe
        The sponsoring organization may prescribe a con-
        vention card on which partners are to list their con-
        ventions, and may establish regulations for its use.
    2. Referring to Opponents' Convention Card
        During the auction and play, any player except
        dummy may refer to his opponents' convention card
        at his own turn to call or play.

CHAPTER VI

The Play

PART I

PROCEDURE

SECTION ONE

CORRECT PROCEDURE

LAW 41

COMMENCEMENT OF PLAY

A. The Opening Lead
   After the auction closes, the defender on declarer's left makes the opening lead.
B. Spreading Dummy's Hand
   After the opening lead has been made*, dummy spreads his hand in front of him on the table. The cards are face up, sorted in suits, with trumps to dummy's right.
C. Playing Dummy's Hand
   Declarer plays both his hand and that of dummy.
D. Inquiry as to Final Contract
   After it is too late to have previous calls restated, as

---

*The sponsoring organization may specify a delay (see footnote to Law 45).

provided in Law 20, declarer or either defender is entitled to be informed as to what the contract is and whether, but not by whom, it was doubled or redoubled.

LAW 42

DUMMY'S RIGHTS

A. Absolute Rights
    1. Give or Obtain Information
        Dummy is entitled to give or obtain information, in the Director's presence, as to fact or law.
    2. Keep Track of Tricks
        He may keep count of tricks won and lost by each side and may draw attention to the fact that another player's card, played to any preceding trick, has been pointed in the wrong direction.
    3. Play as Declarer's Agent
        He may play the cards of the dummy as declarer's agent and only as directed by him (see Law 16).

B. Qualified Rights
    Dummy may exercise other rights subject to the limitations provided in Law 43.
    1. Revoke Inquiries
        Dummy may question players regarding revokes as provided in Law 61 (he may ask a player who has failed to follow suit to a trick whether he has a card of the suit led).
    2. Attempt to Prevent Irregularity
        He may try to prevent any irregularity (he may, for example, warn declarer against leading from the wrong hand).
    3. Draw Attention to Irregularity
        He may draw attention to any irregularity, but only after play of the hand is concluded.

LAW 43

DUMMY'S LIMITATIONS

A. Limitations On Dummy
  1. General Limitations
    (a) Calling the Director
        Dummy should not call the Director during play.
    (b) Calling Attention to Irregularity
        Dummy may not call attention to an irregularity during play except to try to prevent an irregularity before it occurs (Law 42 B2).
    (c) Participate in or Comment on Play
        Dummy may not participate in the play or make any comment on the bidding or play.
  2. Limitations Carrying Specific Penalty
    (a) Exchanging Hands
        Dummy may not exchange hands with declarer.
    (b) Leave Seat to Watch Declarer
        Dummy may not leave his seat to watch declarer's play of the hand.
    (c) Look at Defender's Hand
        Dummy may not, on his own initiative, look at the face of a card in either defender's hand.
B. Penalties for Violation
  1. General Penalties
     Dummy is liable to penalty under Law 86 for any violation of the limitations listed in 'A1' or 'A2' preceding.
  2. Specific Penalties
     If dummy, after violation of the limitations listed in 'A2' preceding:
    (a) Draws Attention to Defender's Irregularity
        Is the first to draw attention to a defender's irregularity, declarer may not enforce any penalty for the offense.

(b) Warns Declarer on Lead

Warns declarer not to lead from the wrong hand, (penalty) either defender may choose the hand from which declarer shall lead.

(c) Asks Declarer about Possible Irregularity

Is the first to ask declarer if a play from declarer's hand constitutes a revoke or failure to comply with a penalty, declarer must substitute a correct card if his play was illegal, and the penalty provisions of Law 64 apply.

LAW 44

SEQUENCE AND PROCEDURE OF PLAY

A. Lead to a Trick

The player who leads to a trick may play any card in his hand (unless he is subject to restriction after an irregularity committed by his side).

B. Subsequent Plays to a Trick

After the lead, each other player in turn plays a card, and the four cards so played constitute a trick. (For the method of playing cards and arranging tricks see Law 65.)

C. Requirement to Follow Suit

In playing to a trick, each player must follow suit if possible. This obligation takes precedence over all other requirements of these Laws.

D. Inability to Follow Suit

If unable to follow suit, a player may play any card (unless he is subject to restriction after an irregularity committed by his side).

E. Tricks Containing Trumps

A trick containing a trump is won by the player who has contributed to it the highest trump.

F. Tricks Not Containing Trumps

A trick that does not contain a trump is won by the player who has contributed to it the highest card of the suit led.

G. Lead to Tricks Subsequent to First Trick

The player who has won the trick leads to the next trick.

LAW 45

CARD PLAYED

A. Play of Card from a Hand

Each player except dummy plays a card by detaching it from his hand and facing* it on the table immediately before him.

B. Play of Card from Dummy

Declarer plays a card from dummy by naming the card, after which dummy picks up the card and faces it on the table. In playing from dummy's hand declarer may, if he prefers, pick up the desired card himself.

C. Compulsory Play of Card

1. Defender's Card

A defender's card held so that it is possible for his partner to see its face must be played to the current trick (if the defender has already made a legal play to the current trick, see Law 45E).

2. Declarer's Card

Declarer must play a card from his hand held face up, touching or nearly touching the table, or maintained in such a position as to indicate that it has been played.

---

*Sponsoring organizations may require an opening lead face down.

3. Dummy's Card

   A card in the dummy must be played if it has been deliberately touched by declarer except for the purpose of arranging dummy's cards, or of reaching a card above or below the card or cards touched.

4. Named or Designated Card

   (a) Play of Named Card

   A card must be played if a player names or otherwise designates it as the card he proposes to play.

   (b) Correction of Inadvertent Designation

   A player may, without penalty, change an inadvertent designation if he does so without pause for thought; but if an opponent has, in turn, played a card that was legal before the change in designation, that opponent may withdraw without penalty the card so played and substitute another (see Law 47F).

5. Penalty Card

   A penalty card must be played, subject to Law 50.

D. Card Misplayed by Dummy

If dummy places in the played position a card that declarer did not name, the card must be withdrawn if attention is drawn to it before each side has played to the next trick, and a defender may withdraw (without penalty) a card played after the error but before attention was drawn to it (see Law 47F).

E. Fifth Card Played to Trick

1. By a Defender

   A fifth card contributed to a trick by a defender becomes a penalty card, subject to Law 50, unless the Director deems that it was led, in which case Laws 53 or 56 apply.

2. By Declarer

   When declarer contributes a fifth card to a trick from his own hand or dummy, there is no penalty unless the Director deems that it was led, in which case Law 55 applies.

F. Dummy Indicates Card

   After dummy's hand is faced, dummy may not touch or indicate any card (except for purpose of arrangement) without instruction from declarer. If he does so, the Director should be summoned forthwith. The Director should rule whether dummy's act did in fact constitute a suggestion to declarer, and if it did (penalty) he may forbid declarer to make any play predicated upon the suggestion.

G. Turning the Trick

   No player should turn his card face down until all four players have played to the trick.

SECTION TWO

IRREGULARITIES IN PROCEDURE

LAW 46

INCOMPLETE OR ERRONEOUS CALL OF CARD FROM DUMMY

A. Proper Form for Designating Dummy's Card

   When calling a card to be played from dummy, declarer should clearly state both the suit and the rank of the desired card.

B. Incomplete or Erroneous Call

   In case of an incomplete or erroneous call by declarer of the card to be played from dummy the following restrictions apply:

   1. Incomplete Designation of Rank

      If declarer, in playing from dummy, calls "high", or words of like import, he is deemed to have called the highest card of the suit indicated (or if dummy is last to follow suit to the trick, the lowest winning card); if he calls "low", or words of like import, he is deemed to have called the lowest.

2. Name of Suit but Not Rank

   If declarer names a suit but not a rank, he is deemed to have called the lowest card of the suit indicated (unless this was incontrovertibly not his intention).

3. Name of Rank but Not Suit

   If declarer names a rank but not a suit:

   (a) In Leading

   Declarer is deemed to have continued the suit in which dummy won the preceding trick, provided there is a card of the named rank in that suit.

   (b) All Other Cases

   In all other cases, declarer must play a card from dummy of the named rank if he can legally do so; but if there are two or more such cards that can be legally played, declarer must designate which is intended.

4. Designated Card Not in Dummy

   If declarer calls a card that is not in dummy, the call is void and declarer may designate any legal card.

5. No Suit or Rank Designated

   If declarer indicates a play without naming either a suit or rank (as by saying, "play anything", or words of like import), either defender may designate the play from dummy except when such play was incontrovertibly not declarer's intention.

LAW 47

RETRACTION OF CARD PLAYED

A. To Comply with Penalty

   A card once played may be withdrawn to comply with a penalty (but see Law 49).

B. To Correct an Illegal Play

A played card may be withdrawn to correct an illegal play (but see Law 49).

C. To Change an Inadvertent Designation

A played card may be withdrawn without penalty after a change of designation as permitted by Law 45C4(b).

D. Following Opponent's Change of Play

After an opponent's change of play, a played card may be withdrawn without penalty to substitute another card for the one played.

E. Change of Play Based on Misinformation

1. Lead Out of Turn

A lead out of turn may be retracted without penalty if the leader was mistakenly informed by an opponent that it was his turn to lead.

2. Declarer's Retraction of Play

(a) Defender Has Not Subsequently Played

Declarer may retract a card played from his own hand or dummy after a mistaken explanation of a defender's conventional play and before a corrected explanation, but only if no card was subsequently played to that trick.

(b) One or More Subsequent Plays Made

When it is too late for declarer to correct a play, under (a) preceding, Law 40C applies.

F. Exposure of Retracted Card by Damaged Side

If a card retracted under sections D or E preceding gave substantial information to an opponent, the Director may award an adjusted score.

G. Illegal Retraction

Except as provided in 'A' through 'E' preceding, a card once played may not be withdrawn.

PART II

PENALTY CARD

LAW 48

EXPOSURE OF DECLARER'S CARDS

A. Declarer Exposes a Card

Declarer is not subject to penalty for exposing a card, and no card of declarer's or dummy's hand ever becomes a penalty card. Declarer is not required to play any card dropped accidentally.

B. Declarer Faces Cards

1. After Opening Lead Out of Turn

When declarer inadvertently faces his cards after an opening lead out of turn, Law 54 applies (but it is a violation of propriety for declarer to spread his hand when he knows he is declarer).

2. At Any Other Time

When declarer faces his cards at any time other than immediately after an opening lead out of turn, he may be deemed to have made a claim or concession of tricks, and Law 68 then applies.

LAW 49

EXPOSURE OF A DEFENDER'S CARDS

Whenever a defender faces a card on the table, holds a card so that it is possible for his partner to see its face, or names a card as being in his hand, before he is entitled to do so in the normal course of play or application of law, (penalty) each such card becomes a penalty card (Law 50); but see Law 70 (Defender's Claim or Concession of Tricks).

LAW 50

DISPOSITION OF PENALTY CARD

A. Definition of Penalty Card

A card prematurely exposed by a defender is a penalty card unless the Director designates otherwise.

B. Penalty Card Remains Exposed

A penalty card must be left face up on the table immediately before the player to whom it belongs, until it is played or until an alternate penalty has been selected.

C. Leader's Partner Has Penalty Card

1. Lead Must Be Held for Declarer's Option

When a defender has the lead while his partner has a penalty card, he may not lead until declarer has stated which of the options open to him he is selecting. If the defender leads prematurely, he is subject to penalty under Law 49.

2. Declarer's Options

(a) Require or Prohibit Lead of Penalty Card Suit

The declarer may require that defender to lead the suit of the penalty card, or may prohibit him from leading that suit for as long as he retains the lead. If declarer exercises this option, the penalty card may be picked up.

(b) Penalty Card to Remain Penalty Card

If declarer does not exercise the option provided in '(a)' preceding, the defender may lead any card, but the penalty card remains a penalty card.

(c) Two or More Penalty Cards

See Law 51.

D. Play of Penalty Card

A penalty card must be played at the first legal opportunity, whether in leading, following suit, discarding or trumping. If a defender has two or more penalty cards that can legally be played, declarer may designate which is to be played. The obligation to follow suit, or to comply with a lead or play penalty, takes precedence over the obligation to play a penalty card, but the penalty card must still be left face up on the table and played at the next legal opportunity.

LAW 51

TWO OR MORE PENALTY CARDS

A. Defender's Turn to Play
   (See Law 50: If a defender has two or more penalty cards that can legally be played, declarer may designate which is to be played at that turn.)

B. Leader's Partner Has Two or More Penalty Cards
   1. Penalty Cards in Same Suit
      (a) Declarer Requires Lead of That Suit
          When a defender has two or more penalty cards in one suit, and declarer requires the defender's partner to lead that suit, the defender may pick up every penalty card in that suit and may make any legal play to the trick.
      (b) Declarer Prohibits Lead of That Suit
          If the declarer prohibits the lead of that suit, the defender may pick up every penalty card in that suit and may make any legal play to the trick.
   2. Penalty Cards in More Than One Suit
      (a) Declarer Requires Lead of a Specified Suit
          When a defender has penalty cards in more than one suit, declarer may require the defender's partner to lead any suit in which the defender has a penalty card (but 'B 1(a)' preceding then applies).

(b) Declarer Prohibits Lead of Specified Suits

When a defender has penalty cards in more than one suit, declarer may prohibit the defender's partner from leading every such suit; but the defender may then pick up every penalty card in every suit prohibited by declarer, and make any legal play to the trick.

LAW 52

FAILURE TO LEAD OR PLAY A PENALTY CARD

A. Defender Fails to Play Penalty Card

When a defender fails to lead or play a penalty card as required by Law 50, he may not, on his own initiative, withdraw any other card he may have played.

B. Defender Plays Another Card

1. Play of Card Accepted

(a) Declarer May Accept Play

If a defender has led or played another card when he could legally have led or played a penalty card, declarer may accept such lead or play.

(b) Declarer Must Accept Play

Declarer must accept such lead or play if he has thereafter played from his own hand or dummy.

(c) Penalty Card Remains Penalty Card

If the played card is accepted under either '(a)' or '(b)' preceding, the unplayed penalty card remains a penalty card.

2. Play of Card Rejected

Declarer may require the defender to substitute the penalty card for the card illegally played or led. Every card illegally led or played by the defender in the course of committing the irregularity becomes a penalty card.

PART III

IRREGULAR LEADS AND PLAYS

SECTION ONE

LEAD OUT OF TURN

LAW 53

LEAD OUT OF TURN ACCEPTED

A. Lead Out of Turn Treated as Correct Lead
Any lead faced out of turn may be treated as a correct lead. It becomes a correct lead if declarer or either defender, as the case may be, accepts it (by making a statement to that effect), or if the player next in rotation plays* to the irregular lead. (If no acceptance statement or play is made the Director will require that the lead be made from the correct hand.)

B. Wrong Defender Plays Card to Declarer's Irregular Lead
If the defender at the right of the player from whose hand the lead out of turn was made plays* to the irregular lead, the lead stands and Law 57 applies.

C. Proper Lead Made Subsequent to Irregular Lead
If it was properly the turn to lead of an opponent of the player who led out of turn, that opponent may make his proper lead to the trick of the infraction without his card being deemed played to the irregular lead. When this occurs, the proper lead stands, and all cards played in error to this trick may be withdrawn without penalty (see Law 47F).

---

*But see "C" below.

LAW 54

OPENING LEAD OUT OF TURN

A. Declarer Accepts Lead

When a defender faces the opening lead out of turn declarer may accept the irregular lead as provided in Law 53, and dummy is spread in accordance with Law 41.

1. Declarer Plays Second Card

The second card to the trick is played from declarer's hand.

2. Dummy Has Played Second Card

If declarer plays the second card to the trick from dummy, dummy's card may not be withdrawn except to correct a revoke.

B. Declarer Must Accept Lead

If declarer may have seen any of dummy's cards (except cards that dummy may have exposed during the auction and that were subject to Law 23), he must accept the lead.

C. Declarer Begins to Spread His Hand

If declarer inadvertently* begins to spread his hand as though he were dummy, and in so doing exposes one or more cards, and if subsection 'B.' preceding does not apply, the lead must be accepted, declarer must spread his entire hand and dummy becomes declarer.

D. Declarer Refuses Opening Lead

When declarer requires the defender to retract his opening lead out of turn, Law 56 applies.

---

*Declarer should, as a matter of propriety, refrain from spreading his hand when he knows that he is declarer.

LAW 55

DECLARER'S LEAD OUT OF TURN

A. Declarer's Lead Accepted

If declarer has led out of turn, either defender may accept the lead as provided in Law 53.

B. Declarer Required to Retract Lead

1. Defender's Turn to Lead

If declarer has led when it was a defender's turn to lead, and if either defender requires him to retract such lead, declarer restores the card led in error to the proper hand without penalty.

2. Lead in Declarer's Hand or Dummy's

If declarer has led from the wrong hand when it was his turn to lead from his hand or dummy's and if either defender requires him to retract the lead, he withdraws the card led in error. He must lead from the correct hand and, (penalty) if able to do so, a card of the same suit.

C. Failure to Comply with Penalty

Failure by declarer to comply with the lead penalty may subject him to penalty under Law 64.

LAW 56

DEFENDER'S LEAD OUT OF TURN

A. Declarer Accepts Lead

See Laws 53 and 54.

B. Declarer Requires Retraction of Lead

When declarer requires a defender to retract his lead out of turn, the card illegally led becomes a penalty card, and Law 50 applies.

SECTION TWO

OTHER IRREGULAR LEADS AND PLAYS

LAW 57

PREMATURE LEAD OR PLAY BY DEFENDER

A. Premature Lead or Play to Next Trick
When a defender leads to the next trick before his partner has played to the current trick, or plays out of turn before his partner has played, (penalty) the card so led or played becomes a penalty card, and declarer must select one of the following options. He may require the offender's partner:
  1. Follow Suit with Highest Card
     To play the highest card he holds of the suit led, or
  2. Follow Suit with Lowest Card
     To play the lowest card he holds of the suit led, or
  3. Play Card of Another Suit
     To play a legal card of another suit specified by declarer.
B. Offender's Partner Cannot Comply with Penalty
When offender's partner is unable to comply with the penalty selected by declarer, he may play any card, as provided in Law 59.
C. Declarer Has Played from Both Hands before Irregularity
A defender is not subject to penalty for playing before his partner if declarer has played from both hands; but a singleton, or one of two or more equal cards (cards of the same suit adjacent in rank) in dummy, is not considered automatically played unless dummy has played the card or has illegally suggested that it be played (see Law 45).

LAW 58

SIMULTANEOUS LEADS OR PLAYS

A. Play Made Simultaneously with Legal Play

A lead or play made simultaneously with another player's legal lead or play is deemed to be subsequent to it.

B. Defender Plays Two Cards Simultaneously

1. Only One Card Visible

If a defender leads or plays two or more cards simultaneously, and if only one such card is visible, he must play that card.

2. More Than One Card Exposed

If more than one card is exposed, he must designate the card he proposes to play, and each other card exposed becomes a penalty card (Law 50).

C. Declarer Plays Two or More Cards Simultaneously

1. Declarer Must Designate Correct Card

If declarer leads or plays two or more cards simultaneously from either hand, he must designate the card he proposes to play, and must restore any other card to the correct hand.

2. Declarer Withdraws Visible Card

If declarer withdraws a visible card and a defender has already played to that card, such defender may, without penalty, withdraw his card and substitute another (see Law 47F).

D. Error Not Discovered

If the error remains undiscovered until both sides have played to the next trick, Law 67 applies.

LAW 59

INABILITY TO LEAD OR PLAY AS REQUIRED

A player may play any correct card if he is unable to lead or play as required to comply with a penalty, whether because he holds no card of the required suit, or because he has only cards of a suit he is prohibited from leading, or because of his obligation to follow suit.

LAW 60

PLAY AFTER AN ILLEGAL PLAY

A. Play of Card after Irregularity
   1. Forfeiture of Right to Penalize
      A play by a member of the non-offending side after the opponent on his right has led or played out of turn or prematurely, and before a penalty has been assessed, forfeits the right to penalize that offense.
   2. Irregularity Legalized
      Once the right to penalize has been forfeited, the illegal play is treated as though it were legal (except as provided in Law 53) unless it constitutes a revoke.
   3. Other Penalty Obligations Remain
      If the offending side had a previous obligation to play a penalty card, or to comply with a lead or play penalty, the obligation remains at future turns (see Laws 52 and 64).
B. Defender Plays before Required Lead by Declarer
   When a defender plays a card after declarer has been required to retract his lead out of turn from either hand, but before declarer has led from the correct hand, the defender's card becomes a penalty card (Law 50).

C. Play by Offending Side before Assessment of Penalty
A play by a member of the offending side before a penalty has been assessed does not affect the rights of the opponents and may itself be subject to penalty.

SECTION THREE

THE REVOKE

LAW 61

FAILURE TO FOLLOW SUIT — INQUIRIES
CONCERNING A REVOKE

A. Definition of Revoke
Failure to follow suit in accordance with Law 44, or failure to lead or play, when able, a card or suit required by law or specified by an opponent in accordance with an agreed penalty, constitutes a revoke (but see Law 59).

B. Right to Inquire about a Possible Revoke
Any player, including dummy (subject to Law 43), may ask a player who has failed to follow suit whether he has a card of the suit led (but a claim of revoke does not warrant inspection of quitted tricks, except at the Director's specific instruction — see Law 66).

LAW 62

CORRECTION OF A REVOKE

A. Revoke Must Be Corrected

A player must correct his revoke if he becomes aware of the irregularity before it becomes established.

B. Correcting a Revoke

To correct a revoke, the offender withdraws the card he played in revoking and follows suit with any card.

1. Defender's Card

A card so withdrawn becomes a penalty card (Law 50) if it was played from a defender's unfaced hand.

2. Declarer's or Dummy's Card, Defender's Faced Card

The card may be replaced without penalty if it was played from declarer's or dummy's hand*, or if it was a defender's faced card.

C. Subsequent Cards Played to Trick

1. By Non-offending Side

Each member of the non-offending side may, without penalty, withdraw any card he may have played after the revoke but before attention was drawn to it (see Law 47F).

2. By Partner of Offender

Except as provided in subsection 'D.' following, the partner of the offender may not withdraw his card unless it too constituted a revoke (in which case, the card withdrawn becomes a penalty card if it was played from a defender's unfaced hand).

D. Revoke after Eleventh Trick

1. Must Be Corrected

After the eleventh trick, a revoke, even if established, must be corrected if discovered before all four hands have been returned to the board.

---

*Subject to Law 43. A claim of revoke does not warrant inspection of quitted tricks except as permitted in Law 67.

2. Offender's Partner Had Not Played to Trick Twelve
   If the revoke occurred before it was the turn of the offender's partner to play to the twelfth trick, (penalty) declarer or either defender, as the case may be, may then require the offender's partner to play to that trick either of the two cards he could legally have played.

LAW 63

ESTABLISHMENT OF A REVOKE

A. Revoke Becomes Established
   A revoke becomes established:
   1. Offending Side Leads or Plays to Next Trick
      When the offender or his partner leads or plays to the following trick (any such play, legal or illegal, establishes the revoke).
   2. A Member of Offending Side Indicates a Lead or Play
      When the offender or his partner names or otherwise designates a card to be played to the following trick.
   3. Member of Offending Side Makes a Claim or Concession
      When a member of the offending side makes a claim or concession of tricks orally or by facing his hand (or in any other fashion).

B. Revoke May Not Be Corrected
   Once a revoke is established, it may no longer be corrected (except as provided in Law 62 D), and the trick on which the revoke occurred stands as played.

LAW 64

PROCEDURE AFTER ESTABLISHMENT OF A REVOKE

A. Penalty Assessed
1. Offending Side Has Won Revoke Trick

   When a revoke is established, and the trick on which the revoke occurred was won by the offending side, (penalty) after play ceases, the trick on which the revoke occurred, plus one of any subsequent tricks won by the offending side, are transferred to the non-offending side.

2. Offending Side Did Not Win Revoke Trick

   When a revoke is established and the trick on which the revoke occurred was not won by the offending side (penalty) after play ceases, one of any subsequent tricks won by the offending side is transferred to the non-offending side.

B. No Penalty Assessed
1. Offending Side Fails to Win Revoke Trick or Subsesequent Trick

   The penalty for an established revoke does not apply if the offending side did not win either the revoke trick or any subsequent trick.

2. Second Revoke in Same Suit by Offender

   The penalty does not apply to a subsequent revoke in the same suit by the same player.

3. Revoke by Failure to Play a Faced Card

   The penalty does not apply if the revoke was made in failing to play any card faced on the table or belonging to a hand faced on the table, including a card from dummy's hand.

4. After Non-offending Side Calls to Next Deal

   The penalty does not apply if attention was first drawn to the revoke after a member of the non-offending side has made a call on a subsequent deal.

5. After Round Has Ended

   The penalty does not apply if attention was first drawn to the revoke after the round has ended.

6. Revoke after Eleventh Trick

   The penalty does not apply to a revoke that was made after the eleventh trick.

C. Director Responsible for Equity

   When, after any established revoke, including those not subject to penalty, the Director deems that the non-offending side is insufficiently compensated by this Law for the damage caused, he should assign an adjusted score.

PART IV

TRICKS

LAW 65

ARRANGEMENT OF TRICKS

A. Completed Trick

   When four cards have been played to a trick, each player turns his own card face down on the edge of the table before him.

B. Keeping Track of the Ownership of Tricks

   1. Tricks Won

      If the player's side has won the trick, the card is pointed lengthwise toward his partner.

   2. Tricks Lost

      If the opponents have won the trick, the card is pointed lengthwise toward the opponents.

C. Orderliness Required

Each player should arrange his own cards in an orderly overlapping row in the sequence played, in order to permit review of the play after its completion, if necessary to determine the number of tricks won by each side or the order in which the cards were played.

D. Agreement on Results of Play

A player should not disturb the order of his played cards until agreement has been reached on the number of tricks won.

E. Noncompliance

1. Rights Placed in Jeopardy

A player who fails to comply with the provisions of this Law may jeopardize his right to claim ownership of doubtful tricks or to claim a revoke.

2. Cards Incorrectly Pointed

Any player may request that a card incorrectly pointed be turned in the proper direction.

LAW 66

INSPECTION OF TRICKS

A. Current Trick

So long as his side has not led or played to the next trick, declarer or either defender may, until he has turned his own card face down on the table, require that all cards just played to the trick be faced for his inspection.

B. Quitted Tricks

Thereafter, until play ceases, quitted tricks may not be inspected (except at the Director's specific instruction, for example, to verify a claim of a revoke).

C. After the Conclusion of Play

After play ceases the played and unplayed cards may be inspected to settle a claim of a revoke, or of the number of tricks won or lost (or of honors in total point play); but no player should handle cards other than his own. If, after a claim has been made, a player mixes his cards in such a manner that the Director can no longer ascertain the facts, the issue must be decided in favor of the other side.

LAW 67

DEFECTIVE TRICK

A. **Irregularity Detected before Both Sides Have Played to Next Trick**

When a player has omitted to play to a trick, or has played too many cards to a trick, the error must be rectified if attention is drawn to the irregularity before a player on each side has played to the following trick.

1. **Player Failed to Play Card**

   To rectify omission to play to a trick, the offender supplies a card he can legally play.

2. **Player Contributed Too Many Cards**

   (a) **Offender Withdraws Surplus Card(s)**

   To rectify the error of playing too many cards, the offender withdraws all but one card, leaving a card he can legally play. Each card so withdrawn becomes a penalty card (Law 50) if it was played from a defender's unfaced hand.

   (b) **Change of Play by Non-offenders**

   After a card has been so withdrawn, each member of the non-offending side may, without penalty, withdraw any card he played after the irregularity but before attention was drawn to it (see Law 47F).

B. Irregularity Discovered after Both Sides Play

When attention is drawn to a defective trick after both sides play to the following trick, or when the Director later determines that there was a defective trick, from the fact that one player holds too few or too many cards and a corresponding improper number of played cards on the table before him, the defective trick stands as played and:

1. Player with Too Few Cards

A player with too few cards plays the remainder of his hand with fewer cards than the other players; he does not play to the final trick (or tricks), and if he wins a trick with his last card the lead passes in rotation.

2. Player with Too Many Cards

A player with too many cards plays the remainder of his hand with more cards than the other players; all cards remaining unplayed after the final trick are added to that trick (but no card so contributed changes the ownership of that trick).

3. Penalty on Offending Player

When it is no longer possible to rectify a defective trick, failure to play a card to that trick, or the play of more than one card to that trick, is penalized as an established revoke. The Director should apply the penalty provisions and exemptions of Law 64. For this purpose the Director should attempt to determine the exact trick at which the irregularity took place, but should he be unable to do so with certainty, the defective trick is deemed to be the earliest one possible.

PART V

CLAIMS AND CONCESSIONS

LAW 68

DECLARER'S CLAIM OR CONCESSION OF TRICKS

A. Concession by Declarer
    Declarer makes a concession when he announces that he
    will lose all of the remaining tricks, or when he agrees to
    a defender's claim.

B. Claim by Declarer
    Declarer makes a claim whenever he announces that he
    will win or lose one or more of the remaining tricks, or
    suggests that play be curtailed, or intentionally faces his
    hand.

C. Required Statement by Declarer
    In making his claim declarer is required to state his
    proposed line of play.

D. Play Ceases
    Play ceases. When declarer has made a claim questioned
    by either defender the Director must be summoned
    immediately. No action of any kind may be taken pend-
    ing the Director's arrival (all play subsequent to a
    claim or concession must be voided by the Director).
    See Law 69.

LAW 69

DIRECTOR'S RULING ON DECLARER'S CONTESTED CLAIM

A. General Objective

In ruling on a contested claim by declarer, the Director should adjudicate the result of the board as equitably as possible to both sides, but any doubtful points should be resolved in favor of the defenders. He should proceed as follows.

B. Investigatory Steps Director Should Follow
   1. Require Declarer to Repeat Claim Statement
      The Director should require declarer to repeat the statement he made at the time of his claim.
   2. Require All Hands to be Faced
      Next, the Director should require all players to put their remaining cards face up on the table.
   3. Hear Defenders' Objections
      The Director should then hear the defenders' objections to the claim.

C. There Is an Outstanding Trump

When a trump remains in one of the defenders' hands, the Director should award a trick or tricks to the defenders if:
   1. Failed to Mention Trump
      Declarer, in making his claim, made no statement about that trump, and
   2. Was Probably Unaware of Trump
      It is at all likely that declarer at the time of his claim was unaware that a trump remained in a defender's hand, and
   3. Could Lose a Trick to the Trump
      A trick could be lost to that trump by any normal play (including the careless or inferior but not the irrational).

D. Declarer Proposes a New Line of Play
   The Director should not accept from declarer any proposed line of play inconsistent with his statement.

E. Declarer Failed to Make Appropriate Announcement
   If declarer did not make an appropriate announcement at the time of his original claim, the Director should not accept from him any proposed line of play the success of which depends upon finding either opponent with or without a particular card, unless an opponent failed to follow to the suit of that card before the claim was made, or would subsequently fail to follow to that suit on any conceivable line of play.

LAW 70

DEFENDER'S CLAIM OR CONCESSION OF TRICKS

A. Defender's Claim
   A defender makes a claim when he announces that he will win one or more of the remaining tricks, or when he shows any or all of his cards to declarer for this purpose.

1. Claim Pertains Only to Current Trick
   If the claim pertains only to an uncompleted trick currently in progress, play proceeds normally; cards exposed or otherwise revealed by the defender in making his claim do not become penalty cards, but Law 16 may apply; and see Law 57.

2. Claim Pertains to Subsequent Tricks
   (a) Play Ceases
       If the claim pertains to subsequent tricks, play must cease (any play subsequent to a claim or concession must be voided by the Director), and the defender is required to state his proposed line of defense.

    (b) Claim Questioned

        When the claim is questioned by declarer, the Director must be summoned immediately and no action of any kind may be taken pending his arrival. The Director should adjudicate the result of the board as equitably as possible to both sides, but should award to the declarer any trick that the defenders could lose by normal (including the inferior or careless but not the irrational) play.

B. Defender's Concession

  A defender makes a concession when he agrees to declarer's claim, or when he announces that he will lose one or more of the remaining tricks. (Concession cancelled, see Law 71.)

LAW 71

CONCESSION CANCELLED

A concession may be cancelled by the Director:

A. Illegal Concessions

    1. Trick Side Has Won

      *If any player concedes a trick his side has, in fact, won.

    2. Contract Fulfilled

      *If declarer concedes defeat of a contract he has already fulfilled.

    3. Contract Defeated

      *If a defender concedes the fulfillment of a contract his side has already defeated.

---

*For a concession to be cancelled under this clause, the error must be reported to the Director within the correction period established under Law 75.

B. Concession of Trick That Cannot Be Lost
    If a trick that has been conceded cannot be lost by any
    probable play of the remaining cards, and if the Di-
    rector's attention is drawn to that fact before all four
    hands have been returned to the board.

C. Concession Disputed by Other Defender
    If a defender concedes one or more tricks and his partner
    immediately objects, but Law 16 may apply.

CHAPTER VII

Proprieties

PART I

GENERAL PRINCIPLES

A. Observance of Laws
   1. General Obligation on Contestants
      Duplicate bridge tournaments should be played in strict accordance with the Laws.
   2. Waiving of Penalties
      In duplicate tournaments it is improper to waive a penalty for an opponent's infraction even if one feels that one has not been damaged.
   3. Non-offenders' Exercise of Legal Options
      When these Laws provide the innocent side with an option after an irregularity committed by an opponent, it is proper to select that action most advantageous.
   4. Offenders' Options
      After the offending side has paid the prescribed penalty for an inadvertent infraction, it is proper for the offenders to make any call or play advantageous to their side, even though they thereby appear to profit through their own infraction.
   5. Responsibility for Enforcement of Laws
      The responsibility for penalizing irregularities and redressing damage rests solely upon the Director and these Laws, not upon the players themselves.

B. Infraction of Law
   1. Intentional
      To infringe a law intentionally is a serious breach of propriety, even if there is a prescribed penalty that one is willing to pay. The offense may be the more serious when no penalty is prescribed.
   2. Inadvertent Infraction
      There is no obligation to draw attention to an inadvertent infraction of law committed by one's own side.
   3. Concealing an Infraction
      A player should not attempt to conceal an inadvertent infraction, as by committing a second revoke, concealing a card involved in a revoke, or mixing the cards prematurely.

PART II

IMPROPER INFORMATION

A. Proper Communication between Partners
   1. How Effected
      Communication between partners during the auction and play should be effected only by means of the calls and plays themselves.
   2. Correct Form for Calls
      Calls should be made in a uniform tone without special emphasis or inflection, and without undue haste or hesitation (however, sponsoring organizations may require mandatory pauses, as on the first round of the auction, or following a skip bid).
   3. Correct Form for Plays
      Plays should be made without emphasis, gesture or mannerism, and so far as possible at a uniform rate.

B. Improper Communication between Partners

   1. Gratuitous Information

      It is improper for communication between partners to be effected through the manner in which calls or plays are made, through extraneous remarks or gestures, or through questions asked of the opponents or explanations given to them.

   2. Prearranged Improper Communication

      The gravest possible offense against propriety is for a partnership to exchange information through prearranged methods of communication other than those sanctioned by these Laws. The penalty imposed for infraction is normally expulsion from the sponsoring organization.

C. Player Receives Improper Information from Partner

   When a player has available to him improper information from his partner's remark, question, explanation, gesture, mannerism, special emphasis, inflection, haste or hesitation, he should carefully avoid taking any advantage that might accrue to his side.

D. Variations in Tempo

   1. Inadvertent Variations

      Inadvertently to vary the tempo or manner in which a call or play is made does not in itself constitute a violation of propriety, but inferences from such variation may properly be drawn only by an opponent, and at his own risk.

   2. Intentional Variations

      It is grossly improper to attempt to mislead an opponent by means of remark or gesture, through the haste or hesitancy of a call or play (such as a hesitation before the play of a singleton), or by the manner in which the call or play is made.

E. Deception

   Any player may properly attempt to deceive an opponent through a call or play (so long as the deception is not protected by concealed partnership understanding). It is entirely proper to avoid giving information to the opponents by making all calls and plays in unvarying tempo and manner.

F. Violation of Proprieties

When a violation of the proprieties described in this part results in damage to an innocent opponent,

1. Player Acts on Improper Information

If the Director determines that a player chose from among logical alternative actions one that could reasonably have been suggested by his partner's tempo, manner or remark, he should award an adjusted score (see Law 16).

2. Player Injured by Deliberate Improper Deception

If the Director determines that an innocent opponent has drawn a false inference from deliberately and improperly deceptive information, he should award an adjusted score (see Law 12).

PART III

CONDUCT AND ETIQUETTE

A. Proper Attitude

1. Courtesy Toward Partner and Opponents

A player should maintain at all times a courteous attitude toward his partner and opponents.

2. Etiquette of Word and Action

A player should carefully avoid any remark or action that might cause annoyance or embarrassment to another player, or might interfere with the enjoyment of the game.

3. Conformity to Proper Procedure
   Every player should follow uniform and correct procedure in calling and playing, since any departure from correct standards may disrupt the orderly progress of the game.

B. Etiquette
   As a matter of courtesy a player should refrain from:

   1. Lack of Attention
      Paying insufficient attention to the game (as when a player obviously takes no interest in his hand, or frequently requests a review of the auction).

   2. Making Gratuitous Comments
      Making gratuitous comments during the play as to the auction or the adequacy of the contract.

   3. Prematurely Detaching a Card
      Detaching a card from his hand before it is his turn to lead or play.

   4. Disorder in Played Cards
      Arranging the cards he has played to previous tricks in a disordered manner, or mixing his cards before the result of the deal has been agreed upon.

   5. Questionable Claims or Concessions
      Making a claim or concession of tricks if there is any doubt as to the outcome of the deal.

   6. Prolongation of Play
      Prolonging play unnecessarily for the purpose of disconcerting the other players.

   7. Disrespectful Summoning of the Director
      Summoning the Director in a manner discourteous to him or to the other contestants.

C. Breaches of Propriety
   It is a breach of propriety:

   1. Variations in Calls
      To use different designations for the same call.

   2. Displaying Reaction to Calls or Plays
      To indicate any approval or disapproval of a call or play.

3. Revealing Expectation of Trick Result

   To indicate the expectation or intention of winning or losing a trick that has not been completed.

4. Pertinent Comment or Act during Auction or Play

   To comment or act during the auction or play to call attention to a significant incident thereof, or to the state of the score, or to the number of tricks still required for success.

5. Volunteering Information

   To volunteer information that should be given only in response to a question.

6. Staring at Other Players

   To look intently at any other player during the auction or play, or at another player's hand as for the purpose of seeing his cards or observing the place from which he draws a card (but it is not improper to act on information acquired by inadvertently seeing an opponent's card).

7. Deliberate Variation of Tempo

   To vary the normal tempo of bidding or play for the purpose of disconcerting the other players.

8. Unnecessary Departure from Table

   To leave the table needlessly before the round is called.

PART IV

PARTNERSHIP AGREEMENTS

A. Concealed Partnership Agreements

It is improper to convey information to partner by means of a call or play based on special partnership agreement, whether explicit or implicit, unless such information is fully and freely available to the opponents (see Law 40).

B. Violations of Partnership Agreements

It is not improper for a player to violate an announced partnership agreement, so long as his partner is unaware of the violation (but habitual violations within a partnership may create implicit agreements, which must be disclosed). No player has the obligation to disclose to the opponents that he has violated an announced agreement; and if the opponents are subsequently damaged, as through drawing a false inference from such violation, they are not entitled to redress.

C. Answering Questions on Partnership Agreements

When explaining the significance of partner's call or play in reply to an opponent's inquiry (see Law 20), a player should disclose all special information conveyed to him through partnership agreement or partnership experience; but he need not disclose inferences drawn from his general bridge knowledge and experience.

D. Correcting Errors in Explanation

1. Explainer Notices Own Error

If a player subsequently realizes that his own explanation was erroneous or incomplete, he should immediately call the Director (who will apply Law 21 or Law 40C).

2. Error Noticed By Explainer's Partner

It is improper for a player whose partner has given a mistaken explanation to correct the error immediately, or to indicate in any manner that a mistake has been made (he must not take any advantage of the unauthorized information so obtained). He is under no legal or moral obligation at any later time to inform the opponents that the explanation was erroneous.*

---

*Two examples may clarify responsibilities of the players (and the Director) after a misleading explanation has been given to the opponents. In both examples following, North has opened one notrump and South, who holds a weak hand with long diamonds, has bid two diamonds, intending to sign off; North explains, however, in answer to West's inquiry, that South's bid is strong and artificial, asking for major suits.

Example 1 - Mistaken Explanation

The actual partnership agreement is that two diamonds is a natural sign-off; the mistake was in North's explanation. This explanation is an infraction of law, since East-West are entitled to an accurate description of the North-South agreement (when this infraction results in damage to East-West, the Director should award an adjusted score). If North subsequently becomes aware of his mistake, it is to his advantage immediately to notify the Director - this may serve to minimize the damage caused by his infraction. **South** must do nothing to correct the mistaken explanation during the auction period; if he becomes declarer or dummy, he may then volunteer a correction of the explanation.

Example 2 - Mistaken Bid

The partnership agreement is as explained - two diamonds is strong and artificial; the mistake was in South's bid. Here there is no infraction of law, since East-West did receive an accurate description of the North-South agreement; they have no claim to an accurate description of the North-South **hands.** (Regardless of damage, the Director should allow the result to stand.) South must not correct North's explanation (or notify the Director) immediately, and he has no responsibility to do so subsequently.

In both examples, South, having heard North's explanation, knows that his own two diamond bid has been misinterpreted. This knowledge is "improper information" (see Proprieties, Part II), so South must be careful not to base subsequent actions on this information (if he does, the Director should award an adjusted score). For instance, if North rebids two notrump South has the improper information that this bid merely denies a four-card holding in either major suit; but South's responsibility is to act as though North had made a strong game try opposite a weak response, showing maximum values.

PART V

SPECTATORS

A. Conduct During Bidding or Play
   1. Personal Reaction
      A spectator must not display any reaction to the bidding or play while a hand is in progress (as by shifting his attention from one player's hand to another's).
   2. Mannerisms or Remarks
      During the round, a spectator must refrain from mannerisms or remarks of any kind (including conversation with a player).
   3. Consideration for Players
      A spectator must not in any way disturb a player.
B. Spectator Participation
   A spectator may not call attention to any irregularity or mistake, nor speak on any question of fact or law except by request of the Director.

CHAPTER VIII

The Score

LAW 72

DUPLICATE CONTRACT BRIDGE SCORING

A. Authorized Scoring

The Rubber Bridge scoring table applies to Duplicate Bridge with exceptions noted as follows:

B. Exceptions

1. Trick Points

Trick points scored on one board do not count toward making game on a board subsequently played.

2. Premium Points

Premium points are scored for making a part-score or game, not for winning a rubber.

3. Honors

Honors are not scored in matchpoint or international-matchpoint play.

LAW 73

DUPLICATE BRIDGE SCORING TABLE

THE SCORE

TRICK SCORE

Scored by declarer's side if the contract is fulfilled.

IF TRUMPS ARE	♣	♢	♡	♠
For each odd trick bid and made				
Undoubled	20	20	30	30
Doubled	40	40	60	60
Redoubled	80	80	120	120

	AT A NOTRUMP CONTRACT		
	UNDOUBLED	DOUBLED	REDOUBLED
For the first odd trick bid and made	40	80	160
For each additional odd trick	30	60	120

A trick score of 100 points or more, made on one board, is GAME. A trick score of less than 100 points is a PART-SCORE.

PREMIUM SCORE
Scored by declarer's side:

SLAMS

	Not Vulnerable	Vulnerable
For making a SLAM		
Small Slam (12 tricks) bid and made	500	750
Grand Slam (all 13 tricks) bid and made	1000	1500

OVERTRICKS

	Not Vulnerable	Vulnerable
For each OVERTRICK		
(tricks made in excess of contract)		
Undoubled	Trick Value	Trick Value
Doubled	100	200
Redoubled	200	400

PREMIUMS FOR GAME, PART-SCORE, FULFILLING CONTRACT

For making GAME, vulnerable	500
For making GAME, not vulnerable	300
For making any PART-SCORE	50
For making any doubled or redoubled contract	50

HONORS
Scored by either side at total-point play, not at matchpoint play:

For holding four of the five trump HONORS (A, K, Q, J, 10) in one hand	100
For holding all five trump HONORS (A, K, Q, J, 10) in one hand	150
For holding all four ACES in one hand at a notrump contract	150

UNDERTRICK PENALTIES
Scored by declarer's opponents if the contract is not fulfilled:

UNDERTRICKS
(tricks by which declarer falls short of the contract)

	Not Vulnerable			Vulnerable		
	Undoubled	Doubled	Redoubled	Undoubled	Doubled	Redoubled
For first undertrick	50	100	200	100	200	400
For each additional undertrick	50	200	400	100	300	600

LAW 74

METHODS OF SCORING

A. Matchpoint Scoring
    In matchpoint scoring each contestant is awarded, for scores made by different contestants who have played the same board and whose scores are compared with his: two scoring units (matchpoints or half matchpoints) for each score inferior to his, one scoring unit for each score equal to his, and zero scoring units for each score superior to his.

B. International Matchpoint Scoring
    In international matchpoint scoring, on each board the total point difference (not including honors) between the two scores compared is converted into IMP's according to the following scale:

Difference in points	I.M.P.	Difference in points	I.M.P.	Difference in points	I.M.P.
20 - 40	1	370 - 420	9	1500 - 1740	17
50 - 80	2	430 - 490	10	1750 - 1990	18
90 - 120	3	500 - 590	11	2000 - 2240	19
130 - 160	4	600 - 740	12	2250 - 2490	20
170 - 210	5	750 - 890	13	2500 - 2990	21
220 - 260	6	900 - 1090	14	3000 - 3490	22
270 - 310	7	1100 - 1290	15	3500 - 3990	23
320 - 360	8	1300 - 1490	16	4000 & upwards	24

C. Total Point Scoring
    In total point scoring, the net total point score (including honors) of all boards played is the score for each contestant.

D. Special Scoring Methods
    Special scoring methods are permissable, if approved by the Sponsoring Organization. In advance of any contest the Sponsoring Organization should publish conditions of contest detailing conditions of entry, methods of scoring, determination of winners, breaking of ties, etc.

LAW 75

TRICKS WON

A. Agreement on Tricks Won

   The number of tricks won should be agreed upon before all four hands have been returned to the board.

B. Disagreement on Tricks Won

   If a subsequent disagreement arises, the Director must be called. No correction may be made unless the Director is called before the round has ended (see Laws 8 and 71).

C. Error in Score

   1. Correction Period Specified

      An error in computing or tabulating the agreed-upon score, whether made by a player or scorer, may be corrected until the expiration of the period specified for such corrections by the sponsoring organization.

   2. Correction Period Not Specified

      Unless otherwise specified by the sponsoring organization, the correction period expires 30 minutes after the official score has been completed and made available for inspection.

CHAPTER IX

Tournament Sponsorship

LAW 76

SPONSORING ORGANIZATION

A sponsoring organization conducting an event under these Laws has the following duties and powers:

A. Tournament Director

To appoint the tournament Director. If there is no tournament Director, the players should designate one of their own number to perform his functions.

B. Advance Arrangements

To make advance arrangements for the tournament, including playing quarters, accommodations, and equipment.

C. Session Times

To establish the date and time of each session.

D. Conditions of Entry

To establish the conditions of entry.

E. Supplementary Regulations

To publish or announce regulations supplementary to, but not in conflict with, these Laws.

CHAPTER X

Tournament Director

SECTION ONE

RESPONSIBILITIES

LAW 77

DUTIES AND POWERS

A. Official Status
   The director is the official representative of the sponsoring organization.

B. Restrictions and Responsibilities
   1. Technical Management
      The director is responsible for the technical management of the tournament.
   2. Observance of Laws and Regulations
      The director is bound by these Laws and by supplementary regulations announced by the sponsoring organization.

C. Director's Duties and Powers
   The director's duties and powers normally include the following:
   1. Assistants
      To appoint assistants, as required to perform his duties.
   2. Entries
      To accept and list entries.
   3. Conditions of Play
      To establish suitable conditions of play, and to an-

nounce them to the contestants.

4. Discipline

   To maintain discipline and to insure the orderly progress of the game.

5. Law

   To administer and interpret these Laws.

6. Errors

   To rectify any error or irregularity of which he becomes aware.

7. Penalties

   To assess penalties when applicable.

8. Waiver of Penalties

   To waive penalties, at his discretion, upon the request of the non-offending side.

9. Disputes

   To adjust disputes, and to refer disputed matters to the appropriate committee when required.

10. Scores

    To collect scores and tabulate results.

11. Reports

    To report results to the sponsoring organization for official record.

D. Delegation of Duties

   The Director may delegate any of the duties listed in 'C' to assistants, but he is not thereby relieved of responsibility for their correct performance.

LAW 78

RECTIFICATION OF ERRORS OF PROCEDURE

A. Director's Duty

   It is the duty of the Director to rectify errors of procedure and to maintain the progress of the game in a manner that is not contrary to these Laws.

B. Rectification of Error
   To rectify an error in procedure the Director may:
   1. Assignment of Adjusted Score
      Assign an adjusted score as permitted by these Laws.
   2. Specify Time of Play
      Require or postpone the play of a board.
   3. Reservation of Decision
      Reserve his decision on any point of fact or law.

LAW 79

NOTIFICATION OF THE RIGHT TO APPEAL

If the Director believes that a review of his decision on a point of fact or exercise of his discretionary power might be in order (as when he assigns an adjusted score under Law 12), he should advise a contestant of his right to appeal.

SECTION TWO

RULINGS

LAW 80

RULINGS ON AGREED FACTS

When the Director is called to rule upon a point of law, procedure or propriety, in which the facts are agreed upon, he should rule as follows:

A. No Penalty

If no penalty is prescribed by law, and there is no occasion for him to exercise his discretionary powers, he should direct the players to proceed with the auction or play.

B. Penalty Under Law

If a case is clearly covered by a law that specifies a penalty for the irregularity, he should assess that penalty and see that it is paid.

C. Player's Option

If a law gives a player a choice from among two or more penalties, the Director should explain the options and see that a penalty is selected and paid.

D. Director's Option

If the law gives the Director a choice between a specified penalty and the award of an adjusted score, he should attempt to restore equity, resolving any doubtful point in favor of the non-offending side.

E. Discretionary Penalty

If an irregularity has occurred for which no penalty is assessed by law, the Director may award an adjusted score.

LAW 81

RULINGS ON DISPUTED FACTS

When the Director is called upon to rule upon a point of law, procedure or propriety, in which the facts are not agreed upon, he should proceed as follows:

A. Director's Assessment

If the Director is satisfied that he has ascertained the facts, he should rule accordingly.

B. Facts Not Determined

If the Director is unable to determine the facts to his satisfaction, he must make a ruling that will permit play to continue, and notify the players of their right to appeal.

SECTION THREE

CORRECTION OF IRREGULARITIES

LAW 82

ADJUSTED SCORE IN TEAM PLAY

A. Normal Play Possible

When an irregularity occurs in team play, if these Laws provide a rectification that will permit normal play of the board, the Director should rule accordingly.

B. Normal Play Impossible

When no rectification will permit normal play of the board:

1. Time Available

If time permits, the Director should substitute a new board to be played at both tables:

(a) Equal Fault

When neither team is at fault or if both teams have contributed to the error, or

(b) Board Not Played

When the teammates of the players involved have not yet played the board.

2. No Time Available

When time will not permit the substitution of a new board, the Director should assign an adjusted score.

3. Board Played at Other Table

When the board has been played at the other table, the Director should assign an adjusted score, taking into consideration in his adjustment any unusually favorable result obtained by the non-offending team.

LAW 83

FOULED BOARD

A. Definition

A board is considered to be 'fouled' if the Director determines that one or more cards were misplaced in the board, in such manner that contestants who should have had a direct score comparison did not play the board in identical form.

B. Scoring the Fouled Board

In scoring a fouled board the Director determines as closely as possible which scores were made on the board in its correct form, and which in the changed form. He divides the score on that basis into two groups, and rates each group separately as provided in the regulations of the sponsoring organization.

SECTION FOUR

PENALTIES

LAW 84

AWARD OF INDEMNITY POINTS

In a pair or individual event, when a non-offending contestant is required to take an adjusted score through no fault or choice of his own, such contestant should be awarded a minimum of 60% of the matchpoints available to him on that board, or the percentage of matchpoints he earned on boards actually played during the session, if that percentage was greater than 60%.

LAW 85

PENALTIES IN INDIVIDUAL EVENTS

In individual events, the Director should enforce the penalty provisions of these Laws, and the provisions requiring the award of adjusted scores, equally against both members of the offending side, even though only one of them may be responsible for the irregularity. But the Director, in awarding adjusted scores, should not assess procedural penalty points against the offender's partner, if, in the Director's opinion, he is in no way responsible for the violation.

LAW 86

PROCEDURAL PENALTIES

A. Director's Authority

The Director, in addition to enforcing the penalty provisions of these Laws, should also assess penalties for any offense that unduly delays or obstructs the game, inconveniences other contestants, violates correct procedure, or requires the award of adjusted scores.

B. Offenses Subject to Penalty

Offenses subject to penalty include but are not limited to:

1. Tardiness

   Arrival of a contestant after the specified starting time.

2. Slow Play

   Any unduly slow play by a contestant.

3. Loud Discussion

   Any discussion of the bidding, play, or result of a board, which may be overheard at another table.

4. Comparing Scores

   Any comparison of scores with another contestant during a session.

5. Touching Another's Cards

   Any touching or handling of cards belonging to another player (Law 7).

6. Misplacing Cards in Board

   Placing one or more cards in an incorrect pocket of the board.

7. Errors in Procedure

   Any error in procedure (such as failure to count cards in one's hand, playing the wrong board, etc.) that requires an adjusted score for any contestant.

8. Failure to Comply
   Any failure to comply promptly with tournament regulations, or with any instruction of the Director.
9. Improper Behavior
   Any improper or discourteous behavior.

LAW 87

SUSPENSION AND DISQUALIFICATION OF PLAYERS

A. Director's Power to Suspend
   In performing his duty to maintain order and discipline, the Director is specifically empowered to suspend a player for the current session or any part thereof (the Director's decision under this clause is final).

B. Director's Right to Disqualify
   The Director is specifically empowered to disqualify a player, pair or team for cause, subject to approval by the Tournament Committee or sponsoring organization.

CHAPTER XI

Appeals

LAW 88

RIGHT TO APPEAL

A. Contestant's Right
    A contestant may appeal for a review of any ruling made
    by the Director or by one of his assistants.
B. Time of Appeal
    Any appeal of a Director's ruling must be made not later
    than thirty (30) minutes after the conclusion of the
    session during which the ruling was made.
C. How to Appeal
    All appeals must be made through the Director
D. Concurrence of Appellants
    An appeal shall not be heard unless both members of a
    pair (except in an individual contest), or the captain of a
    team, concurs in appealing. An absent member shall be
    deemed to concur.

LAW 89

PROCEDURES OF APPEAL

A. No Appeals Committee
    The Chief Director should hear and rule upon all appeals
    if there is no Tournament or Appeals committee, or
    when a committee cannot meet without disturbing the
    orderly progress of the tournament.

B. Appeals Committee Available

If a committee is available,

1. Appeal Concerns Law

The Chief Director should hear and rule upon such part of the appeal as deals solely with the law. His ruling may be appealed to the committee.

2. All Other Appeals

The Chief Director must refer all other appeals to the committee for adjudication.

3. Adjudication of Appeals

In adjudicating appeals the committee may exercise all powers assigned by these Laws to the Director, except that the committee may not overrule the Director on a point of law or regulations, or on exercise of his disciplinary powers.

C. Appeal to National Authority

After the preceding remedies have been exhausted, further appeal may be taken to the national authority (on a point of law, in the ACBL the National Laws Commission, 2200 Democrat Road, Memphis, TN 38116).